TRIBAL DEMOGRAPHY OF GONDS

TRIBAL DEMOGRAPHY OF GONDS

By

Dr. B.G. Banerjee
Miss Kiran Bhatia

GYAN

ISBN : 978-81-212-0237-4

Published, 2018

Published by

Gyan Publishing House
5, Ansari Road
Daryaganj, New Delhi-110002
Phone: 011-47034999, 9811692060
www.gyanbooks.com
E-mail: books@gyanbooks.com

Printed at: G. Print Process, Delhi.

Preface

According to the 1981 census, the tribal population of India comprising over three hundred communities was 51.63 million persons, constituting 7.76% of India's total population. Madhya Pradesh, Orissa, Bihar and Rajasthan account for 60% of the entire Scheduled Tribal population in the country. However, the detailed demographic data on most of the tribal populations are lacking.

While demography as such is comparatively a new discipline, tribal demography can hardly be assessed to have crossed the stage of infancy. One is reminded of Wattal's book *Population Problem in India* (1934) and his mention of 'Fertility of Animists' (a term used for the tribal societies). "India's Population—Facts and Policy", published in 1946 by Chandra Sekhar, had a couple of pages on aboriginal population. It must be admitted that it was Mamoria who for the first time in 1957 brought out a book exclusively devoted to tribal demography in India.

The raison d'etre for undertaking a study on tribal demography is to be sought in the planned development of the Scheduled Tribes to a very large extent. Some academic interest was generated side by side during the decade 1950-60.

However, one of the major factors that gave positive direction to the demographic studies on the tribals was the publication of 1961 series monographs on Scheduled tribes by Indian census organisation. Later Roy Burman and Nag addressed themselves to the problems of tribals including population policy and family planning.

It is unfortunate that many established departments of anthropology and sociology in various universities and institution do not impart a basic course in tribal demography. In an era of planned development, the significance of tribal, demography, as a distinct specialization of social demography, can hardly be ignored. An urgent need was felt to have a text dealing exclusively with Tribal Demography based on intensive fieldwork. To begin with, we thought, nothing could be more befitting than making a micro-level study of Gonds, one of the largest tribal populations of India.

The authors owe a profound sense of gratitude to Professor Dr. S.R.K. Chopra, Vice-Chancellor of Kurukshetra University, Kurukshetra who has been a constant source of inspiration and moral support. Dr. V. Bhalla and Dr. S. Prakash of Department of Anthropology, Panjab University, Chandigarh, helped the authors at various stages of the work. The authors are indebted to them also.

The authors acknowledge their gratitude to Prof. R.C. Chandna, Department of Geography, Panjab University for his continued interest in the population study. Sincere thanks to Mr. K.C. Kaistha of Department of Sociology and Dr. B.N. Ghosh, Department of Economics, Panjab University, for evincing their interest in the work and for their useful suggestions. The authors are indeed indebted to the faculty members of the department of Anthropology, Panjab University. Drs. R.N. Vashisht, B.S. Karir, S. Kaul and Mr. C.J. Edwin rendered timely help for which the authors are grategul to them. Lastly, the authors are also grateful to Gian-Publising House, Delhi for publishing this book in a short time.

B.G. Banerjee
Kiran Bhatia

Contents

		Page
Preface		v
List of Tables		ix
CHAPTER		
1.	Introduction	1
2.	Development of Social Demography	9
3.	Social Organisation	25
4.	Size, Distribution and Characteristies of Gond Population	47
5.	Demographic Processes	77
6.	Summary	111
	Selected Bibliography	117
	Appendix	125-133
	Index	135-136

List of Tables

		Pages
3.1	Mandla District (Adivasi) population (1981 Census).	27
3.2	Population of Scheduled Tribes in Mandla district (1981 census).	28
3.3	Distribution of Tribal Population in Mandla district (1981 census).	29
3.4	Average birth and death rates in Mandla district.	29
3.5	Distribution of population in Nandia Panchayat (1981 census).	32
3.6	Distribution of population (1971 census).	33
3.7	Clan-wise distribution of households of the village.	34
3.8	Clan-wise distribution of population with respect to household and family size.	35
3.9	Clan-wise distribution of actual and preferred family size among Gonds.	37

3.10 Medical facilities available in Mandla distt. (1984) Hospital & Dispensary 41

3.11 Distance in Km. 42

4.1 Distribution of sex-ratio in India and Madhya Pradesh. 49

4.2 Distribution of Households and sex-wise population of Gonds. 50

4.3 Clan-wise distribution of sex-ratio. 52

4.4 Distribution of population by age and sex. 54

4.5 Dependency ratio. 55

4.6 Population of India and its growth, 1891-1981. 56-57

4.7 Tribal population in India and its growth, 1891-1971. 58

4.8 Tribal population in Madhya Pradesh, 1951-1981. 59

4.9 Marital status of the Gonds of Behanga. 62

4.10 Mean age at marriage by sex in India. 63

4.11 Comparative account of mean age at marriage of different clans of Gonds. 64

4.12 Position of workers and non-workers in India. 66

4.13 Occupational distribution of various clan-groups. 67

4.14 Literacy rate in India by sex and rural urban residence, 1951-1981. 70

4.15 Educational status of different Gond Literates. 72

41.6 Clan-wise literacy among children of age group 5-14 years. 74

5.1 Average decade birth rate in India, 1901-1981. 79

5.2 Average decade birth rate in Madhya Pradesh, 1971-81. 79

5.3	Fertility rate among respondents in different age groups.	80
5.4	Clan-wise crude fertility rate (CFR).	81
5.5	Clan-wise general fertility rate (GFR).	82
5.6	General fertility rate (GFR)	83
5.7	Age specific fertility rate(ASFR).	85
5.8	Gross fertility rate (GFR).	86
5.9	Family Planning among Gonds.	90
5.10	Estimated annual death rates in India, 1881-1981.	93
5.11	Estimated annual death rates in Madhya Pradesh, 1901-1981.	93
5.12	Clan-wise crude death rate.	95
5.13	Age-specific death rate.	96
5.14	Percentage distribution of deaths by major cause groups in rural India 1975-1979.	97
5.15	Infant mortality rates in India, 1911-1971.	99
5.16	Infant mortality rates in Madhya Pradesh, 1941-1970.	100
5.17	Infant mortality rate of Gonds.	100
5.18	Marriage migration in Gonds.	104

APPENDIX

1.	Table showing clan-wise distribution of Gond population by age and sex.	129

2. Table showing clan-wise marital status of Gond-population. 130

3. Table showing population in India, Census (1901-1981.) 131

4. Table showing percentage distribution of live-births by order of birth and area in India (General) and Madhya Pradesh, 1972-1978. 132

5. Table showing average fertility rate, total fertility rate and Gross reproduction rates in India (General) and Madhya Pradesh, 1971-1978. 133

INDIA

DISTRIBUTION OF THE GONDS

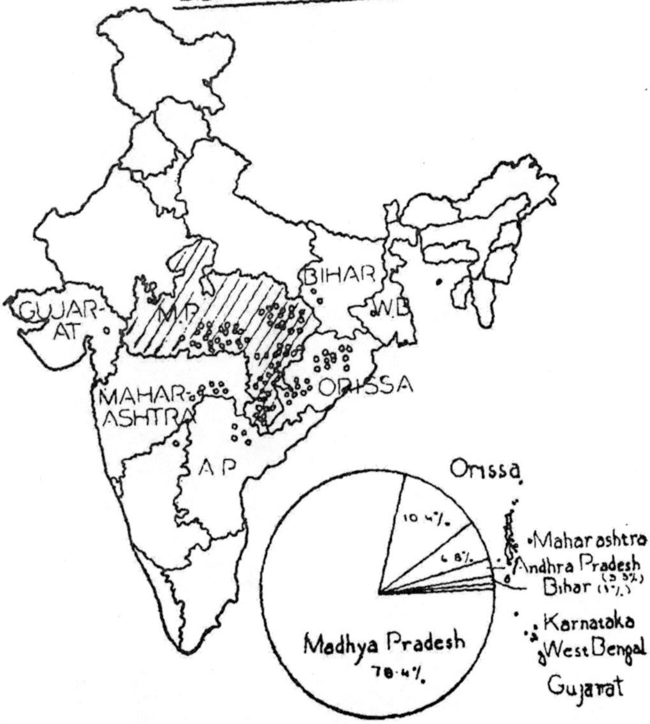

1

Introduction

THE scares of population explosion, that is, enormous increase in numbers from one decade to the next, concentration of population in the metropolitan cities, and very fast expansion of urban areas are matters of great concern. The public, and the social scientists and planners in particular, are being alerted over the past three decades to the 'menace' of rapid world population growth and its consequences with regard to the survival of the human race. But how do we come to know that the population of a country is growing at a very fast rate leading to above problems. These and similar other questions become part and parcel of the field of demography.

World-wide interest in the problems arising from rapid population growth has now become a major concern. India was the first among the few countries that awakened to the need of firm policy of population control and the government promoted family planning programmes right from the First Five-Year Plan. This was because on 2.4 per cent of the land area of the earth, the country had to support almost 15 per cent of the world's population. The absolute increase in our population per annum equals almost the entire population of Australia or Malaysia.

Demography concerns itself with the aggregates of people and their quantification in different ways. The first goal of demography is to determine the size of population. The second is to know what are the proportions of men and women, the age distribution, the distribution of population by marital status, the distribution of workers according to occupations, and so on. And the third to discern the factors which bring changes in the population size.

Definition and Concept

Demography is a science which deals with human populations. The term is derived from two Greek words, *demos*, the people and *graphos*, meaning to draw or write.

Acille Guillard (1855), was the first to popularise the word, demography. He regarded demography as the mathematical knowledge of the general movements and of the physical, social, intellectual and moral conditions of population or still more broadly as the natural social history of humans.

The Multilingual Demographic Dictionary defines demography as the "scientific study of human populations, primarily with respect to their size, their structure and their development" (U.N., 1958:3). Another limited view of demography is taken by Wrong who defines it as "the statistical description and analysis of human populations". (Wrong, 1967).

Economists, biologists, sociologists, anthropologists, geographers, ecologists and statisticians have all contributed to the science of demography. They have taken both the narrow and the broad view of the discipline of demography. A distinction is made between 'demographic analysis' and 'population studies'. Demographic analysis is confined to the study of the components of population variation and change (viz. fertility, mortality and migration). Population studies, on the other hand, are concerned with population variables — social, economic, political, genetic, geographical and the like. Thus, demography is understood in the narrow sense as synonymous with 'demographic analysis' and 'population studies'.

Broad view of Demography: According to Srivastava (1983), Spengler, Vance, Ryder, Lorimer and Barckley prefer to define demography in a broad sense. These writers and many other also regard demography as a multi-disciplinary study or a multiscience discipline. The disciplines of demography, agronomy, economics, sociology, biology, medical sciences, education etc are all considered to be allied to population sciences. They regard the combined coordinated strength of all the professions and sciences as being essential for meeting the realities of the population problems and search for effective and human solutions. In a broad sense, demography includes both 'demographic analysis' and 'population studies'. A broad study of demography includes both qualitative and quantitative aspects of population.

Thus, demography according to the broad view taken by various writers, is the statistical and mathematical study of the size, composition, spatial distribution of human populations and of changes over time in these aspects through the operation of five processes of fertility, mortality, marriage, migration and social mobility. Demography studies the size, composition, distribution of population and change in these aspects through time and examines the causes of these changes.

Narrow view of Demography: A number of demographers, notably Hauser and Duncan (1959), Whipple and others prefer to take a narrow view of the subject. This conventional and narrow view is taken when demography is treated as a branch of anthropology only which deals with statistics of births, deaths and diseases. Demography, thus, becomes a study of 'vital statistics' only.

Hauser and Duncan (1959), are of the opinion that there cannot be an integrated and comprehensive theory. Such a body of theory would have to embrace such diverse pre-occupations as those of economics, social psychology and genetics. In this case the range of the theory or the scope of the frame of references have to be nearly as great as that of the collective totality of the social and life sciences or virtually co-extensive with the natual history of man. Such a position is not acceptable to them. They are of the opinion that demographic explanation about all these problems will have to be completed somewhere. Demography has got to be limited to one discipline.

Hauser and Duncan (1959), have given a working definition of demography as "a study of the size, territorial distribution and composition of population, changes therein, and the components of such changes, which may be identified as mortality, territorial movement (migration) and social mobility (change of status)."

Consensus: A great majority of demographers and planners however, are now more inclined to take a broad view of the definition of demography. Demography is now regarded both as a discipline and technique. Demographic analysis and population studies are both included in the subject. The subject deals with the static as well as the dynamic aspects of population. It is now regarded both as an abstract science and applied technology. With improved data, new techniques and the precise measurement of the demographic transition it has become science rather than literature, that the narrow view of the subject would make it (Srivastava, 1983).

Social Demography

Population studies deal with the inter-relationships of demographic variables with the variables of other disciplines. Social demography in that sense becomes specific in which one relates demographic variables with the variables of the social system.

According to Premi (1983), the use of the term, social demography, has been on the increase in recent years but, as is true of many disciplines, neither the context nor the boundaries of social demography can be defined with exactitude. Conceived in general terms, the major concern of social demography can be said to be the analysis of the inter-relationships of general, social and cultural factors with population structure (size, composition and distribution) and population processes related to dynamic behaviour (fertility, mortality, nuptiality and mobility).

In the study of such inter-relationships, on the one hand, social and cultural factors are viewed as independent variables that account for empirical regularities (or variations) in population size, its structure and processes of change in them; on the other hand, pure demographic variables are treated as independent variables to study the ways in which changes in them affect various aspects of society and culture, as well as social structure. These latter aspects can be represented by 'social action system' (informal groups, associations communities and institutions of marriage and family, religious, political and economic systems and health, education and welfare systems) or by 'social aggregate system' which is made up of characteristics of individuals and groups like race, religion, caste, ethnic background, marital status, family characteristics, education and income as well as attitudes, values and beliefs. This approach to the definition of social demography can be represented by the overlapping areas of the circles representing social action system and social aggregate system with the circles representing demographic system (Fond and De Jong 1970).

According to Premi (1983), diagrammatically, this can be represented in the following manner (see diagram on the next page). In this framework, a social action system is chiefly characterised by the inclusion of various forms of interactions of the systems members. This interaction can be institutionalised through the institutions of marriage and family, religion, economic and political system and health, education and welfare systems, it can be non-institutionalised as well which is represented by informal groups, associations and communities. A basic assumption of sociology is that personal interaction gives rise to social norms which govern social behaviour many times involving basic demographic processes of nuptiality, fertility, mortality and migration and through them, influence demographic structure strongly, affect the nature of personal interaction and, hence, the functioning of social action systems. A study of these inter-relationships becomes an important field of social demography. This is particularly so in India considering its long history and great diversity of cultures and traditions people have in different parts of the country who are living at different levels of economic and social development, from the primitive mode of certain tribal groups to the most complex and sophisticated ways of our great metropolises.

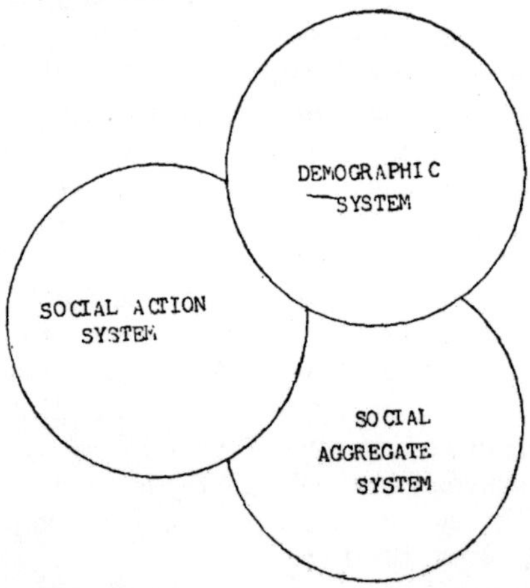

Population size
Composition
Distribution
Fertility
Mortality
Migration

Principal Elements	*Principal Elements Socially defined*
Informal groups	Race
Associations	Ethnic background
Communities	Marital status
Marriage and family	Family characteristics
Institutions	Labour force
Religious institutions	Population
Political institutions	Occupation

Economic institutions	Industry
Health institutions	Education
Welfare institutions	Income
Educational institutions	Religion
	Analytically defined
	Attitudes
	Values
	Beliefs

(After M. K. Premi, *et al* 1983)

The study was made with a view to studying the demographic strutucre of a village, Behanga in District Mandla of Madhya Pradesh. The demographic variables taken into account are population composition, and demographic processes of fertility, mortality, migration and marriage. An account of responses to family welfare programmes was also noted.

Since the area to be investigated was economically backward, illiterate and poverty-stricken, it was hypothesised as under ;

- Number of males and females shall be nearly equal with males outnumbering females at younger age and females outnumbering the males from about the age of 20—25 years onwards, the overall effect being that the females outnumber males to a certain extent.

- The fertility rate is expected to be high.

- Mortality and Infant mortality rates are expected to be high.

- Internal migration, especially inter-state movement shall be minimal. Marriage migration shall be the only way of territorial mobility, extended within a specified short distance.

- The knowledge of family planning and the means of adoption it expected to be low.

To begin with a house- to house contact was intended though the total number of households in the village was 102, yet paucity of time did not permit the investigators to contact all households. Thus, only 69 households (67.6%) were contacted. Refusal of 15-20 households made the task difficult.

A list of households on the basis of census household number was obtained from the Patwari of the village and simple random sampling was done.

The information required was collected from the selected households by administering schedule. The unit of enquiry i.e. 'household' meant all members in a house, who had a common kitchen (*chullah*) and who lived under one roof.

Besides the method schedule and observation, method of interview was also adopted to seek additional information on economic status, family planning and various other aspects.

Before the actual data collection a pilot survey was conducted so as to familiarise with the villagers and establish rapport with them. This survey was done to establish rapport and to win confidence of the people.

2

Development of Social Demography

DEMOGRAPHY, although it may appear to be a new science to many, is in fact one of the oldest social sciences with a history of over three hundred years. The origin of formal demography antedates the development of a systematic population theory by a full century. The term, demography, was first used by Acille Guillard (1855) though John Graunt has the credit of beginning the study of demography in 1662 with the publication of an article in London entitled "National and political observations .... upon the Bills of Mortality". John Graunt was the first exponent of the 'analysis approach' while Thomas Robert Malthus can be said to be the leader of the 'problem-approach' in demography.

Population principles attracted attention of economists, sociologists and statesmen in ancient times. The primitive tribes solved their problem of over-population by infanticide and abortions. Roughly speaking until the end of 16th century the relationship between the birth rates and death rates posed problems since the relation between them was not compatible with the stationary economic environments. Plato and Aristotle observed the possibility of over-population. However, Xenophon never wanted to limit the population. For the achievement of division of labour and prosperity of the city, he recommended a large population. In the middle ages, at some places, overcrowding was observed.

But in the seventeenth and eighteenth centuries under-population became a problem. Some countires, for example Germany and Spain, experienced de-population for decades together. In course of time, anti- populationists sentiment grew in England, although England was having the opposite type of things.

Only in the first decade of the nineteenth century, the data regarding population could became available at regular interval. The earlier writers were ignorant of statistical facts. In the seventeenth and eighteenth centuries, the main task of population research was not to analyse the given facts but to find out what the facts were.

In order to study the population, a number of theories were propounded by different scholars.

Malthusian Theory of Population

Thomas Robert Malthus (1766-1834) was the first person to systematise information in matters of population and initiate a number of views expressed in his first *Essay on the Principle of Population as it Affects the Future Improvements of the Society*- which later came to be known as Malthusian principle of population.

Malthus, on the basis of statistcal data, argued that population has a constant tendency to increase beyond the means of subsistence. He believed that the population has a tendency to multiply in geometric progression i.e. it will increase thus : 1:2:4:8:16:32:64 and so on. Thus it will double in every 25 years. As against the population increase, the food supply has a tendency to increase in arithmetical progression only i.e. food supply will increase as 1:2:3.........and so on.

Since population increases in geometrical progression and the food supply in arithmetical progression, population will outrun food supply. As a result of this imbalance there would be over-population.

Malthus stressed that two types of checks could be used for overgrowing population i.e. preventive checks and positive checks. The preventive checks are applied by men to control birth rate through late marriage, celibacy, moral restraint and foresight whereas the positive checks operate in the form of misery, vice, famine, war, disease, floods and other natural calamities which tend to reduce population, and thereby bring a balance between population growth and the growth of food supply. According to him, positive checks are crude and hence in a civilised society preventive checks are always in operation.

Malthus believed that two of the main characterstics, essential to the maintenance of life were immutable, were natural laws, and were antagonistic.

(i) The need for food.

(ii) The passion between the sexes.

It was the second which led people to marry at a relatively early age and would result in such a large number of births that the population would double itself in a few years if unchecked by misery and vice, and

(iii) Operation of law of diminishing returns in agriculture.

The principle of population enunciated by Malthus did generate a critical review of the issues raised by him. To start with, his basic premise on passion between the sexes has been questioned on the plea that the desire to have children cannot be mixed up with the passion and desire for sex. The desire for sex is a biological instinct, whereas the desire to have childern is a social instinct. Secondly, even the validity of the two sets of ratios has been questioned by his critics. Population has rarely grown in geometrical proportion and means of subsistence have rarely multiplied in arithmetic proportion. Thirdly, the time span of 25 years, assumed by Malthus to allow population to double itself, also does not seem to be anywhere near reality. The doubling period for a population varies from country to country depending upon the stages of its economy, scientific and technological advancement. For instance, it took only 20 years for the population of Mexico to double itself while the population of the U.S.A. took as many as 120 years to register a twofold increase. Fourthly, Malthus also seems to have been swayed away by the supremacy of positive checks over preventive checks mainly because he was thinking about unnatural checks such as delayed or late marriages, moral restraints and controlled frequency of sex after marriage. It is rather strange that Malthus could not think of the use of contraceptives as an effective preventive check. Above all, natural calamities had occurred in under-populated areas as well. Thus there was no causal relationship between positive checks and over-population. Fifthly, Malthus has been severely criticised on his ignoring the rate of changing technology and changes in socio-economic set up of a society. Lastly, he failed to realise even the biological limitation—that, a population cannot grow beyond a certain limit.

Optimum Theory of Population

Several well-known scholars of the twentieth century have propounded the Optimum Theory of Population after being disillusioned with the Malthusian theory of Population. Sidgwick in his *Principles of Political Economy*, laid the foundation of Optimum theory. Later on, Edwin Cannon gave a scientific and systematic orientation to this theory. In recent years Robbins, Dalton, Carr-Saunders have done much to popularise the theory of optimum population. The optimum population approach is concerned with the relation between the size of population and the production of wealth.

The concept of optimum population, according to Dell and Luthringer (1938) implies a population best suited to attain some desired state. This concept of an 'Optimum' has meaning, of course, only if viewed in connection with some assumed purposes or objective. Daltan defines it as the population which gives the maximum income per head. According to Robbins, the population which just makes the maximum returns possible is the optimum or best population. Carr-Saunders defines it as that population which produces maximum economic welfare. Cannon defined the optimum population thus: 'At any given time (in a country) there is what may be called a point of maximum return when the amount of labour is such that both an increase and decrease in it would diminish proportionate returns. If population is not large enough to bring all industry upto this point, returns will be less than they might be and the remedy is increase of population. If on the other hand, population is so great that the point has been passed, returns are again less than they might be and remedy is decrease in population.

The optimum population is that ideal size of population which provides the maximum income per head. Any increase or decrease in the size of population above or below the optimum level will decrease the per capita income.

There are two main assumptions of the optimum theory:

(i) Along with the increase of populations in the country there is no change or unstability in the proportion of total and working population. It means that if there is a change in per capita produce of an average labour, there is also a change in the proportion of per capita income.

(ii) When population increased, there is no change, in the natural resources, volume of capital and technological conditions of the country.

There are two important things which merit our consideration regarding the Optimum Theory of population:

(i) The Optimum population of any country is never stationary, if the means of production are altered numerically and that without the use of definite means for slowing down the rate of growth of population through abortion, infanticide and so forth, man would never have approached the optimum number.

Thus optimum population is an innocuous phrase, optimum has been regarded as a word synonymous with the best.

It is well to recognize the limitations of the optimum theory. The concept is abstract and the problem is complicated. The optimum theory is criticised for its making no allowance for moral and spiritual values in its calculations. The standard adopted is quantitative, ignoring the development of the human personality, the living of the 'good life'. The assessment of values in human life, in terms of their consequences upon productive efficiency alone, is a narrow view of human welfare. Qualitatively, the size of optimum population also alters. So it can rise or fall.

ii) Secondly, it is very difficult to determine the optimum population of any country. In every country the economic forces are constantly changing. There are also changes in the technology of production. Besides changes in the birth and death rates also take place. So it is difficult to determine the population size properly.

Prof. Daltan has given a formula for calculating the over-population and under-population of a country.

$$M=\frac{a-0}{0}$$

Where M= Maladjustment

a= Actual population

o= Optimum population.

The maladjustment is the deviation from the optimum. Maladjustment is a function of two variables-i) the optimum level of population (o) ii) the actual level of population (a) when M is positive, the country is over-populated but if it is negative, the country is under-populated. When M is Zero, the country will be neither under nor over populated and the actual population would be equivalent to optimum population.

Socio-cultural and economic theories of population :

Marxian theory of 'Surplus' population

Karl Marx (1818-1883) was an economist, revolutionary, political thinker, sociologist, and historian. He did not propound any theory of population separately. But his surplus population theory has been deduced from his theory of communism. He vehemently criticised the Malthusian theory of population.

Marxian thrust is on the premise that there are specific laws of population growth for each social system. He declared that there could be no population problem under socialist modes of production and ownership of resources. Population becomes a 'problem' and a part of it becomes 'surplus' only under capitalist modes of production. That part of the population which is excess of the food supply is surplus in economic sense but this is due to maldistribution of resources which condemns men to penury in the midst of plenty.

According to Marx, increase in population in a country is not due to the increase in fertility rate, but it is due to the capitalistic economic system. A capitalist gives to the labour as wage a small share of labour's productivity and keeps the rest of the share for himself. The capitalist introduces more and more machinery and thus increases the surplus value of labour's productivity, which goes into the pockets of capitalist. The surplus value is the difference between labour's productivity and the wage level. A labour is paid less than the value of his productivity when the machinery is introduced, unemployment increases and consequently the reserve army of labour is created. Under these situations wage level goes down further and a large part of population becomes virtually surplus.

According to Marx, poverty and misery were not natural inevitabilities but were the evils of capitalism. He held that the poverty and misery were entirely a consequence of conditions of unemployment and under-employment arising out of the inability of the capitalistic system to provide jobs for all, regardless of the speed with which the population increased. He strongly advocated social reforms to free the society from the evils of capitalism.

Thus Marx had a distinctive approach to the population problem and was able to visualise such transformation of society that could eliminate poverty and misery rather than accept it as a natural inevitability.

It is true that due to the capitalistic method of production a large part of the population becomes surplus, but it is not true to say that in a socialist economy, it is not at all necessary to control the rate of growth of population. Even in a socialist economy, birth rate is being reduced under the pretext of improvement of the health of mothers and their participation in the work of social reconstruction. In fact, even after the eradication of inequality, the socialist countries show different rates of growth of population, and full employment, strictly speaking, is existing nowhere in the world.

Dumont's theory of social capillarity

Arsene Dumont (1849—1902) advanced his theory of social capillarity in depreciation to the theories of population propounded by the Malthusian and political economists. He advocated in his theory that the principle of social capillarity was preceded by two principles, i. e. the Malthusian and the Guillard's principles.

Malthusian theory is applicable to the uncivilised society where human beings live like animals. In such a society, population grows at a geometric rate. When the society is slightly civilised, population grows along with food supply. In such a society, Guillard's theory of population is applicable. This principle says that population grows proportionately with food supply. In such a society, Malthusian positive checks do not become applicable.

This principle is based on the social stratification in a society. It is also recognised that people strive to better their lot in order to attain a particular status in society. This striving includes the pleasures for power and prestige.

In a civilised society Dumont's theory of social capillarity becomes applicable. Every man wants to enhance his social prestige not necessarily for political or economic gains; wealth is not everything, pride and human dignity also counts. Man cannot attain this position with the burden of many children. Children serve as stumbling blocks in the march of man upwards or in social capillarity.

Dumont points out that the low fertility in France has always served as a cause of high intellectual and aesthetic development. It is not the poverty that is the cause of high fertility, it is rather, the remoteness from the urban centres which promotes ignorance and poverty. Poverty is the condition and not the cause of high fertility. Similarly, wealth is not the cause of low fertility. In the urban centes the fertilty is low because of the pronounced social capillarity.

Dumont finds that birth rate is lower in cities and higher in villages. In cities, there are stronger urges for a better standard of living, higher income and wealth, better knowledge, position thinking and rationality and a constant and intense desire for progress and prestige. Due to all these birth rate remains lower. Whereas in the rural areas poverty, ignorance, superstitions, economic motives account for high birth rate.

Socialism is not considered fit, by Dumont, to provide safeguard against population. He opined that the socialist principles of the equality and justice if entirely applied, would, necessarily imply the destruction of social capillarity and cause of high birth rate. Similarly, in a capitalistic society, there are limited opportunities for the common people to rise up to the highest rung of the ladder. Thus, in cepitalism, birth rate connot be lowered.

Frank Fetter's hypothesis of voluntarism

Like other social demographers, Frank Fetter also disagrees with Malthusian ideals of population growth. He admits that man by nature is a complicated social animal. His ideals are always under the influence of his feelings, ideals, desires and will. He needs certain other things to survive instead of mere good. According to Fetter no theory of population covers the matter comprehensively. He, therefore, starts his theory by dividing the society into classes. He recognises the importance of family and takes its function similar in all classes. He does not believe that poor people of the society will limit their families with the fear of food shortage. Reversely, they welcome the birth of a child, because the child, after some years, becomes an earning member and thus adds to the source of family income. On the other hand, the wealthy people are always conscious of limiting their families lest their standard of living should go down. Moreover, unlike the children of poorer sections of the society their children do not become economic assets for quite a long time. Another function which prevents the wealthy people to increase members of their families is the factor of inheritance, the property to be divided among the heirs which might cause the loss of social prestige. Therefore, the well-to-do people maintain prudence and foresight in their reproductive behaviour and the size of their family, whereas the poor hardly care for anything. Thus the issues revolve round the voluntarism of an individual in the society and his environment.

F. S. Nittis principle of individuality

F. S. Nittis (1894) principle of increasing individuality in his book 'Population and the Social System' has been acknowledged well by the thinkers of population science.

Nittis claims to have found out a theory of population which would inflict a death blow to the Malthusian theory. Nittis has given economic, social and biological factors important roles in population growth. According to him, psychological, political, social and moral factors are important in the determination of fertility rates of human beings.

However, the economic factor remains by far the most crucial among these factors. Biological factors are not less important.

Nittis points out that when individuality develops in the society, the inequality with respect to wealth will reduce when the causes of inequality end, and social co-operation increases, population will not increase at a rate more than the rate of growth of food supply.

Therefore, population growth will not be regarded as something alarming and dangerous. The solution of the problem of population, which has been scarcely anything better than utter darkness to economists, is to be found in the biological theory, which has revealed new horizons to demographic science.

Liebenstein's Economic Theory of Population

According to Harvey Liebenstein, the population growth of a nation has four critical points of growth depending upon the income levels. In his book, *Economic Backwardness and Economic Growth*, he has propounded a thesis about the *Critical Minimum Efforts* for lifting an under-developed economy from stagnation. According to him, in the densely populated countries, population growth is an obstacle to economic growth because it dilutes the amount of capital with which the workers work. Increase in population, other things remaining the same, reduce per capita income.

Liebenstein points out that people in backward areas are irrational. They neither know how to check conception nor do they have means or will to check conception. They beget more children as an insurance against high mortality. He gives a cost benefit analysis for extra children.

Every child involves three types of utilities and two types of costs. The utilities are :

(a) A child has a consumption utility (a source of personal pleasure to the parents).

(b) Utility as a productive agent (a source of family income).

(c) Utility as a source of security (in the old age and in difficulties of parents).

Similarly, a child involves direct and indirect costs. The direct costs are the rearing and maintenance cost (cost of feeding, clothing etc). Indirect costs consist of opportunities lost (earning lost during gestation period and during the period of lack of mobility). Three changes that occur during the course of economic development affect the utilities and cost of an additional child. These changes are the income effects, survival effects and the occupational distribution effects.

Leibenstein assumes the 'consumption utility' to be constant, for it cannot be said with certainty that this utility increases with income. He assumes this utility to be constant. Security and production utility functions are assumed to be declining. Costs are certainly a rising function of income. Rich parents bring up their children in costlier ways.

Thus, more rapid the rate of growth, greater is the motivation for family limitation. Liebenstein has found a correlation between per capita income and population growth in the following manner in terms of motivation.

(1) When the income is very low, the mortality rate is very high. Since the death rate is very high, the birth rate has to be high. The utilities from marginal child is very high, whereas the cost of a marginal child is very low (at low income, maintenance cost is low).

(2) When the income increases mortality rate declines but fertility does not decrease immediately, because people immediately do not know that mortality rate has decreased. The productive age of a child becomes lengthier than the non- productive age. Therefore, the direct cost of a child declines. The utilities (as productive agent and as a source of security) of a child increases. Thus fertility does not decrease.

(3) When income increases still more, and more children survive, the utility of a child as a source of protection also decreases. On the other hand, cost of a child increases (both the money and the opportunity cost). Thus fertility tends to decline.

(4) At a very high rate of income, the gap between fertility and mortality gradually reduces. Both fertility and mortality become lower, and country becomes developed.

Leibenstein propounds the thesis that the less the fertility lag the less the critical minimum effect necessary for growth. The point at which fertility decline sets in, will determine the height of the critical minimum income. This level will happen in the second stage, Leibenstein gives us 'motivation theory' of population growth. The rate of population growth is a function of the level of per capita income. At some per capita income level the rate of population growth is the maximum and beyond that point the rate declines.

The Theory of Demographic Transition

The Demographic Transition theory relates the type of population growth to the level of socio-cultural economic and technological development of a society. It is also termed as the modern theory of population. The population condition of a nation is a function of its birth rate and death rate. Birth rate and death rate work in such a way that population growth is either stationary, high or low. Population growth experiences transition from one stage to another which is known as demographic transition.

According to this theory a country has to pass through three stages of population growth.

(i) Period of stable population growth (low population growth).

(ii) Period of rapid population growth and

(iii) The period of stationary or slow population growth.

The period of stability can be a period of high birth rates and high death rates or a period of low birth rates and low death rates. The periods of growth will be periods of rapid, moderate or slow population growth. Though population growth follows certain stages the duration of a particular stage in a country need not be the same. The logistic cause of population growth provided a basis for the theory of demographic transition.

C.P. Blacker (1947) discussed 5 stages of population growth instead of three. These are :

(i) High stationary phase marked by high fertility and mortality rate.

(ii) The early expanding phase marked by high fertility and high but declining mortality.

(iii) Late expanding phase with declining fertility and with mortality declining more rapidly.

(iv) The low stationary phase with low fertility balanced by equally low mortality and

(v) The declining phase with low mortality, lower fertility and an excess of mortality over fertility.

Karl Sax (1950) gave four stages of population growth which are :

(i) High stationary phase marked by high birth rate and high death rate.

(ii) Expanding phase marked by stable birth rate and declining death rate.

(iii) Declining growth of population marked by stable death rate and declining birth rate.

(iv) Stationary phase marked by equal birth and death rates.

Adolphe Landry (1945) also asserts that population growth in a country follows the three stages :

(i) *Primitive Regime* : The population increases with the increase in availability of food grains and declines with the fall in food output. Death rates are directly co-rrelated to increase and decrease in food supply.

(*ii*) *Intermediate population regime* : In this increase in population depends not on the food supply but on the level of economic development. People want to maintain the standard of living and consider increasing number as constraint to development.

(*iii*) *Modern population epoch* : It sees considerable fall in the birth rates and the rate of growth of population cannot be related to either food supply in economic growth.

Donald Olden Cowgill (1949) has conceived five stages of population growth. They are :

(*i*) *Primitive or Malthusian cycle of population growth* : This stage can be explained by Malthusian theory. The brith rate becomes very high and death rate changes according to the natural factors.

(*ii*) *The modern cycle of population growth* : In this stage, the death rate declines more rapidly than the birth rate. Thus, population growth rate increases. However, when the birth rate [and death rate become equal, the rate of growth of population becomes stable.

(*iii*) *Future cycles—baby boom period* : This stage is marked by a stable low death rate and a changing birth rate. The birth rate generally becomes higher than the death rate. This peaiod has been called by Cogwill 'a period of baby boom'.

(*iv*) *A probable cycle* : It is marked by high death rate and a high birth rate, but birth rate increasing more rapidly than the death rate. Therefore, the rate of growth of population becomes rapid.

(*v*) *Population cycle in the long run* : According

to Cogwill, a rapid rate of growth of population can be explained by a high birth rate and a declining death rates. If the death rate increases but the brith rate declines, population growth will decline. In the long run, the rate of growth of population will depend on the relative effects of birth rates and death rates.

Merits of The Theory of Demographic Transition

The theory of demographic transition is the modern and the most acceptable theory of population growth. It is not based on a relationship between population and food supply as indicated in the Malthusian theory. The Theory of Demographic Transition is superior to the optimum theory which mainly emphasises the increase in par capita income for the growth of population and neglects the other important factors.

The theory of demographic transition is based on the actual trend of the population growth in different phases of economic growth of a country. It is also based on the empirical finding of population growth in different developed countries of Europe. Almost all countries have passed through the first two stages of this theory and are now in the final stage. The theory is equally applicable to all the developing countries as well. A few very backward countries in Africa are still in the first stage, whereas all the other developing countries are in the second stage of transition.

The theory of demographic transition has universal applicability. This theory unlike other theories of population, takes into consideration all the factors—economic, social, biological etc. that influence the growth of population in a country.

3

Social Organisation

Land and People :
Gonds of Madhya Pradesh

The universe of study for the present demographic analysis is village Behanga. It is situated in Mandla district of Madhya Pradesh.

Mandla is situated almost in the centre of Madhya Pradesh at a height of 1200-1400 feet. Jabalpur and Shahdol districts are situated in the northern part of Mandla. The eastern border of Mandla is covered by Bilaspur and Rajnandgao districts. On the southern border is Balaghat district while western part is covered by Sivini district.

The total area covered by Mandla district is 13,257 sq km. It is divided into five Tahsils :

(i) Mandla Tahsil

(ii) Niwas Tahsil

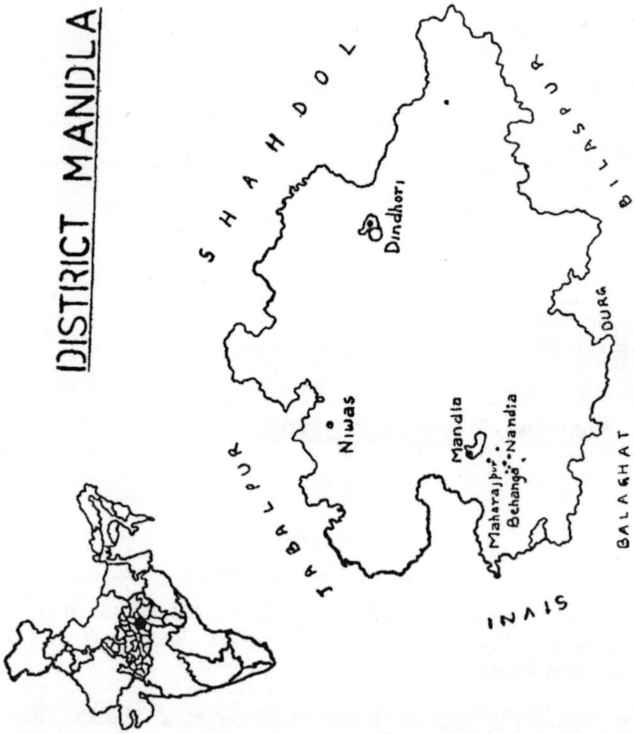
DISTRICT MANDLA
SHAHDOL
BILASPUR
DURG
BALAGHAT
SIVNI
JABALPUR
Dindhori
Niwas
Mandla
Nandia
Maharajpur
Behanga

(iii) Nainpur Tahsil

(iv) Dindhori Tahsil and

(v) Shahpur Tahsil

In all, there are 175 villages in Mandla block and 44 panchayats. The total population of Mandla block, according to 1981 census, is 10,36,134. Amongst the total population, 4289 individuals belong to scheduled castes and 47,477 to scheduled tribes (45% of total population belong to Scheduled Castes and Scheduled Tribes).

TABLE—3.1

Mandla District (Adivasi) Population

Development blocks	Total population	S.C.	S.T.	%
Mandla village area	82,505	3,604	3,746	45.44%
Mandla urban area	27,465	1,056	1,655	36.7%
Nainpur rural area	69,506	3,193	38,627	54.10%
Nainpur urban area	14,683	1,683	1,221	8.37%
Bichia	83,214	3,624	45,324	54.0%
Mavai	46,808	778	34,982	74.13%
Mohgao	40,326	1,532	25,754	63.54%

(Source: Census of India 1981, Madhya Pradesh)

Themajor population of Mandla comprises tribal population. The predominant tribal communities are Gonds, Baiga, Kaul and Pardhans.

TABLE–3.2

Population of Scheduled Tribe in Mandla Districi(1981 Census)

Total population = 5,28,865

S.No.	Division of Scheduled Tribes	Population
1.	Baiga	48,803
2.	Bhaina	2,129
3.	Bhumiya, Bhunihar	1,665
4.	Bhijvar	7
5.	Dhanvar	86
6.	Halwa & Halwi	1
7.	Gond, Agaria,Adar, Badaria etc.	4,34,746
8.	Khadia	2
9.	Korwa	155
10.	Kaul	20,160
11.	Munda	12
12.	Oraon & Dhanika	148
13.	Pardhan, Pathari, & Saroti	16,646
14.	Paradhi and Bahalia	308
15.	Praia	3
16.	Others	1,673

(Source: Office of Census, Mandla district)

TABLE—3.3

Distribution of Tribal Population in Mandla district

(1981 Census)

General population	—	10,36,134
Tribal population	—	6,21,051
% of tribal population	—	59.94%

S.No.	Tribe	Population	Percentages
1.	Gond	5,27,893	85%
2.	Baiga	49,684	8%
3.	Pardhan	31,052	5%
4.	Kaul	3,105	0-5%
5.	Others	9,317	1-5%

(Source: Office of Census, Mandla district.)

According to the census report, Gonds and Baigas are the most significant tribes in this district constituting 93% of the total tribal population of the area. Gonds residing in urban areas of Mandla constitute 13.6% .

In comparison to the other tribes, Gonds are well settled and economically better off than any other communities of the area. Raj Gonds, Nagvanshi Gonds and Ravanvanshi Gonds reside mainly in this area.

The density of population in Mandla district is 78 persons per sq.km. The male-female ratio of this district is almost 1 : 1, according to official reports. The average birth and death rates are given in the following table.

Table—3.4

Average Birth and Deah Rates in Mandla District

	Birth rate	Death rate
Urban	5.07	5.76
Rural	27.07	9.90

(Source: Office of Census, Mandla district)

Gonds in Mandla district

Gonds were earlier mostly forest-dwellers but are at present settled agriculturists and hence are also referred as *Kisan* (farmer). Out of the total population of Gonds, 97% are engaged in agriculture while rest 3% are labourers.

The food habits of Gonds are somewhat uniform. Their staple food is the gruel of millet and boiled rice. Both vegetarian and non-vegetarian foods are common among them. They hardly hesitate to take any kind of meat exception being their respective totemic symbols. Beef-eating is generally restricted, indicating their inclination towards Hinduism.

Gonds follow tribal endogamy and clan exogamy. Monogamous marriage is common among the Gonds but polygamy, is not altogether unknown. Cross-cousin marriage (both paternal and maternal) is preferred. Parallel—cousin marriage has not been observed. They follow the system of patriarchy. Remarriage and widow marriage is also permitted. Divorces are very common among Gonds.

The male Gonds wear *dhoti*, which is kept in position above their knees with a small shirt known as *bandi*. The ladies wear half-sarees which are mostly red, green or blue in colour. They wear loose blouse which is called *Polka*. They wear silver ornaments. Gond women are tattooed generally on the chest. fore-arms, legs, shoulders and ankles. Both men and women used to be tattooed earlier but this custom is constantly on decline among men.

The clans are usually named after some animals or plants. Among the common clans in different districts are *Markam* (mango tree), *Tekam* (teak tree), *Netam* (the dog), *Warkara* (wild cat) and so on. From these animals and plants a clan derives its name and totems for the members of its social group. The totemic association generally has a legendary background.

The religious observances include prohibitions against members of the totemic group, killing or eating the totemic species. Ali (1973) states that "the rule is not always observed, and in some cases they now have some other object of veneration, possibly because they have forgotten the meaning of the sect, name or the object after which it is named has ceased to be sacred".

The worship of ancestors is an integral part of their religion. *Bura Deo*, the great God, was probably at first the *Saj* tree, but afterwards, the whole collection of gods were sometimes called *Bura Deo*. They believe also in a number of local deities.

The dialect used by Gonds is *Gondi*. This dialect is spoken by 21.5% of Gond population.

The tribal area is notorious for veneral diseases, gastric disorders, jaws and skin disorders, scabies and malaria. The incidence of deaths in the area due to malaria was the highest, followed by respiratory diseases, diarrhoea and dysentery.

Health and disease are important for every society, primitive or advanced, and every society has developed its own expedient for treatment and cure of diseases to which it is confronted. Gonds resort to the use of local herbs and medicines independently or through the medicine man, *Gunia*.

The Gonds have a highly developed aesthetic sense. They indulge in merry-making and pleasure seeking which is manifested in dancing and singing and in celebration of festivals like Holi and Megnath swinging rite. Megnath is said to be the son of Ravan, the demon king of Ceylon. They are highly superstitious and are always afraid of 'evil eyes' and other misfortunes like epidemics etc.

The dead person, whether male or female, is buried. He is buried with face upward, head to the north and feet to the south, in clothes in which he died with a new cloth spread over the body. The body is not given a bath before burial.

The influence of various leaders under different situations is also observed. Gonds have a tribal council to settle local disputes of internal nature such as conjugal infidelity and other social matters while they settle the extraneous matters in the presence of *Mukadam* i. e. the village headman.

The exercise of powers by leaders is mostly through the panchayat. Besides economic and political powers, the panchayat also exert administrative rights over the subject. There are 44 panchayats in Mandla block.

The village Behanga covers a total area of 516 hectare, 65 hectare land is coverd by forests. It comprises 83 houses and 128 households. The total population of this village is 813 (according to 1981 census report), out of which 807 persons belong to Scheduled Tribe and the village has a dominating Gond population.

The village is included in Nandia Panchayat. There are 3 other villages which are also included in the same panchayat. The total population included under this panchayat is 1, 678. The population structure of the 4 villages is as follows:

TABLE–3.5

Distribution of Population in Nandia Panchayat (1981 Census)

Village	Scheduled Castes	Scheduled Tribes	General	Total
Nandia	24	141	252	417
Behanga	–	807	6	813
Dhungaria	—	164	38	202
Subharia	–	228	18	246
Total	24	1,340	314	1,678

(Source : Office of Census of India, Mandla)

The village is divided into two tolas (division)—

i) Pateli tola

ii) Kherwa tola.

Table 3.6

Distribution of Population (1971)

Tola	Number of households	Population	Male	Female
Pateli tola	65	486	245	241
Kherwa tola	37	264	129	135

(Source : Office of Census of India, Mandla)

The house types in Behanga are identical for members of all clans. They have *kuccha houses*. The walls of the house are made of mud and grass while the roof is made of *Khaprail* (mud tiles). They have small courtyards in front and back of their houses. The house are spacious, but with no windows or ventilators.

There is one primary school in the village with the total strength of 80. There are two teachers. The Principal of the school, usually referred as *Guruji*, is educated up to 8th class. There is no market, no Post-Office and no health centre in the village. There is no temple in this village. Hand pumps are the only source of drinking water. The village has no electricity facilities.

Agriculture is the only means of their subsistence. The staple food of the villagers is rice (*chawal*), millet (*jawar*) wheat (*ghehu*), maize (*makka*) and pulses (*dal*). Men and women work together in the fields. The men of the village are lazy because of the evils of smoking and drinking. They smoke *chilam hukka* (Hubble-bubble).

Household and Family size

The term household is a basic unit in demography. The term 'household' concerns with all members in a house, who share a common kitchen (*chullah*) and live under a single roof. The demographers consider household as the unit of enquiry. It is because it gives more elaborate description of natural group in which people live.

Table 3.7

Clan-wise Distribution of Households of the village

Clan Group	Total number of household	Total Population	Males	Females
Maravi	20	124	62	62
Warkara	15	97	55	42
Oikey	6	41	19	22
Kushram	2	22	15	7
Chai-devi	2	11	6	5
Dhumkati	1	11	4	7
Neti	7	46	26	20
Partai	10	63	33	30
Wayam	1	10	5	5
Sariyam	1	17	9	8
Sat-devki	2	13	8	5
Sirsam	1	9	5	4
Kurwati	1	10	6	5
Total	69	474	247	127

In Madhya Pradesh, the tribe, Gond, has nearly 45-50 sub-tribes or clans spread over several districts. The total sub-tribes investigated by the investigation in the village are 13. These sub-tribes owe their names to different animals and plants which are referred as totems.

Table 3.7 shows the distribution of these 13 sub-tribes, their distribution of households and the population studied. According to the table, maximum households are of Maravi with a population of 124 and minimum in Sirsam with the population of 9 in one household.

Table 3.8

Clan-wise Distribution of Population with respect to Household and family size

Clan-group	No. of households	Nuclear family house-holds	Extended family households
Maravi	20 (100.00)	15 (75.00)	5 (25.00)
Warkara	15 (100.00)	13 (86.66)	2 (13.33)
Oikey	6 (100.00)	4 (66.66)	2 (33.3)
Kushram	2	2 (100.0)	— (0)
Chai-devki	2	2 (100.0)	— (0)
Dhumkati	1	1 (100.0)	— (0)
Neti	7	6 (85.7)	1 (14.2)
Partai	10	8 (80.0)	2 (20.0)
Wayam	1	1 (100.0)	—
Sat-devki	2	1 (50.0)	1 (50.0)
Sirsam	1	—	1 (100.0)
Kurwati	1	1 (100.0)	—
Sariyam	1	—	1 (100.0)
Total	69	54 (78.26)	15 (21.73)

It is evident from Table 3.8 that both types of family households are found in the village. The number of nuclear and extended families is 54 and 15 respectively. It is clear that extended family system is less prevalent than nuclear family household. Not a single extended household is recorded in Kushram, Chai-devki, Dhumkati, Wayam and Kurwati clans.

In the village the total number of households was 102 out of which 69 households were investigated. In these family households the number of members varies from 2 to 20. Thus, accordingly categories on the basis of size of family are made.

(i) Small family—consisting upto 4 members.

(ii) Medium family—5 to 8 members.

(iii) Large family—9 onwards.

Preferred family size

Associated with the question of desire for sons is the question of preferred family size, which may take the form of 'desired' or 'ideal' size. In the advanced Western societies where planned parenthood is a way of life, data on expected family size have great predictive significance. Even there, family size preferences change with time under the impact of socio-economic changes during the course of married life and to possible fecundity problems. Such changes particularly affect preferences formed early in marriage, as occupational carrier is unfolded and the wife gains experience of child bearing. Bumpass and Westoff (1975), found from their longitudinal study that the number of children desired after the birth of the second child predicts the average completed family size very well. The desire formed at this stage constitute meaningful goals, in terms of which the respondents regulate their subsequent behaviour. However, the position in India is very different. There is a wide gap between the preferred family size and actual family size. Most of the surveys show the preferred size to be three children in urban areas and four in the rural areas, yet large families are most common. The massive propaganda for 3-4 children merely express a group norm, but do not represent a real desire of some intensity and is not a signal for action in practice.

Table 3.9

Clan-wise Distribution of Actual and Preferred family size among Gonds of Behanga

Clan/Sub-Tribe	Preferred family size (Number of children)	Actual family size (Number of children)
Maravi	3-4	4-5
Warkana	3-4	4-5
Oikey	2-3	4-5
Partai	3-4	3-4
Neti	3-4	5-6
Sariyam	3-4	6-7
Sirsani	3-4	4-5
Sat-devki	3-4	4-5
Chai-devki	2-3	4-5
Wayam	2-3	2-3
Kushram	3-4	6-7
Dhumkati	2-3	2-3
Kurwati	3-4	5-6

Table 3.9 gives the actual and preferred family size among Gonds of Behanga. It shows that the actual and preferred size do not tally at all. The actual family size is larger than preferred. The average preferred family size according to the Table is 3-4 whereas the actual family size is 5-6.

Beliefs and Attitudes

Human existence without beliefs and attitudes is virtually inconceivable for it would be an existence without continuity. Beliefs and attitudes can be seen as the building blocks of individual's world and for all practical purposes, the pattern of his beliefs and attitudes may be taken as equivalent to the pattern of his world view.

Krech, Crutchfield and Ballachey (1948) have presented the fact very clearly by maintaining that "the way . man treats .. is determined by his beliefs...his feelings and his dispositions to respond. These cognitions, feelings and action tendencies are inter-related to form a system. This particular system we call his attitudes."

The impact of beliefs and attitudes, on social actions is due to industrial reliance on them. Such reliance is a part of the fundamental economic or least effort principle (Edward and Gerard, 1967). No special rites are observed during pregnancy and the superstitions about women, in this condition they resemble those of the Hindus. A pregnant woman must not go near a horse or an elephant as they think that either of these animals would be excited by her condition and would assault her.

If a child is born with his feet first, its feet are supposed to have special power, and people suffering from pain in the back come and have their backs touched by the toes of the child's left foot. This power is believed to be retained in later life of the child too.

It is believed that if a barren woman can get hold of the first hair of another woman's child on its navel cord, she can transfer the mother's fertility to herself, so they dispose these articles very carefully. If they wish the child to grow fat they bring the navel cord in a manure heap.

The diseases of children are attributed to evil spirits. The illness called *sukhi* in which the body and limbs grow weak and have a dried up appearance, is very common and is probably caused by malnutrition. They attribute it to the machinations of an owl which has heard the child's name or obtained a piece of its soiled clothing. In order to cure this illness they use charms and amulets, and also let the child wallow in a pig-sty so that it may became as fat as pig.

If a Gond, when starting on a journey in the morning, meets a tiger, cat or hare or a four horned deer, he returns and postpones his journey, but if he meets one of these animals when he is well on the way it is considered to be lucky. Rainfall at a wedding on some other festival is unlucky, as it is believed to be someone's cry.

When there is drought two boys put a pestle across their shoulders, tie a living frog to it with a rag, and go from house to house accompanied by other boys and girls singing "Mendak Bhai Pani De" (Brother frog give rain). The frog is considered to be able to produce rain because it lives in water and therefore has control over *its* elements.

Burial of the dead has probably been the general custom of the Gonds in the past, and the introduction of cremation may be ascribed to Hindu influence. The dead are usually buried with the feet pointing to the north in opposition to the Hindu practice, and this fact has been adduced in evidence of the Gond's belief that their ancestors came from the North. The funeral takes place on the second or third day, when these have assembled. Some pieces of cloth, together with the deceased's own clothes and some money, are buried with him, so that they may accompany his spirit to the other world. Children who die when still at breast freeding stage are buried at the roots of a mahua tree, as it is thought that they will suck liquor from them and be nourished as if by their mother's milk.

Diet, Health and Housing

The diet determined by socio-cultural factors has its own sociological significance and therefore in a study of social demography it cannot be ignored as it affects the fecundity and fertility in two ways: directly in the sense that it affects these by its nature and type and indirectly in the sense that it affects the health which, in turn, has its, consequences for fecundity and fertility.

Health and diseases are the measures of effectiveness with which human groups combining biological and cultural measures adapt to their environment (Richard W. Leiban, 1973). Health has been quite often expressed as a disease free state which is somewhat negative statement because health necessarily has a positive implication that has been stressed by

World Health Organization (1950)—"As a state of complete physical, mental and social well-being and not merely the absence of disease or infirmity." Health is a normal and desirable state of existence. Despite rural and tribal areas services having been made compulsory, we still find these regions more or less devoid of any medical care facilities.

The Gonds are extremely poor. They are under-fed, under-nourished and lead a sub-human existence. The situation becomes all the more aggravated when scarcity conditions prevail in these areas and they have to depend on jungle roots and fruit for diet. The malnutrition among tribals make them prone to various diseases like malaria, gastric disorders and tuberculosis.

Among Gonds, Kodo, Kutki, Pej (gruel) and vegetables and tender leaves of trees particularly 'pipal' and certian roots form their diet. They do not spare any animal for the sake of flesh, even snakes and crocodiles are their favourable dish. They like liquor brown from mahua flowers.

Gonds have large variety of edibles but because of their poor economic conditions they have limited access to them. Their staple food is traditional, simple and suited to their economic conditions. The most commonly grown food is millet, Pulses and vegetables, but fats, spices and milk are rare.

The Gonds of the village take their meals three times a day. Early in the morning at about 7.30 or 8.00 A.M. they take breakfast which constitute of starch of rice, Pej (Juara.) In the afternoon at about 2.00 P.M. they take lunch (*marriya*) which includes Pej (*Juara*) and Bhaji (*vegetable*) and after returning from the field, the dinner at about 6.30 or 7.00 P.M. which is called as *Biyari* which constitutes rice (*Bhat kodai*) and Dal or vegetable.

It is evident from the foregoing account that the Gonds are undernourished and lead a subhuman existence. The village has no proper water facilities. Hand pumps and a small nullah water is used for various purposes by the villagers. Since the total number of hand pumps in the whole village is very low, say 2, it is mainly the nullha water which is used.

The houses of Gonds are generally damp, insufficiently ventilated, overcrowded and devoid of the most rudimentary sanitary facilities., which attracts malaria or respiratory diseases etc. Diseases common among the Gonds are malaria, veneral diseases, gastric disorders, skin diseases and tuberculosis. The incidence of malarial fever is mainly responsible for most of the mortality and a large proportion of population suffers from malaria cachxia.

The causes of the diseases may be attributed to imbalanced diet, malnutrition, polluted drinking water and other insanitary unhygienic habits of the Gonds. Abondonment of their original diet in favour of rice diet has caused dysentery and cholera.

Gonds have their own traditional medicines and cures which are effective enough in ordinary diseases, Gonds have more faith in magic cures done by '*gunia*' an '*panda*'. They believe that sickness is caused in most cases by evil spirits or by wrath of gods, who are not worshipped or are neglected. The villagers are still under the influence of the '*ojha*'. For the treatment of boils etc, they practise a gruesome method of pricking them with burning needle. After the birth of the child umbilical cord is normally cut with an unsterilised sickle often leading to tetanus infection. There has been no orientation programmes for the '*Dais*'.

Table 3.10

Medical facilities available in Mandla Distt. (1984)

Hospital & Dispensary

	Allopathic	Pri. Health Centre.	Ayurvedic & Unani	Homeo-pathic	No. of bed
1980-81	1	84	10	1	238
81-82	1	96	12	2	320
82-83	1	80	15	3	334
83-84	1	80	21	3	334

The major problem is the distance between village and Primary Health Centres.

Table 3.11

Distance in Km.

	Nandiya (km)	Dungania (km)	Behanga (km)
Pri. Health Centres	14	17	15
Ayurvedic Hospital	8	10	8
Homeopathic	8	10	8

Due to greater distances of health centres and in the absence of ambulance or other eonveyance facilities lesser number of indviduals were able to make use of medical facilities, than expected.

Normative Practices

Universally, social control in society operates through various norms and their practices such as folkways mores, customs, traditions, institutions, and legal rules and regulations which award for the socially and culturally approved behaviour and punish for the one which is in their contravention.

Norms existing in any social system evolve out of its religious and socio-cultural milieu.

People all over the world have certain occasions on which they have joyful celebrations including the organisation of feasts, music, concerts, plays and the like. These folk-lores and festivals help in removing boredom occurring from the monotony of the routine work. Festivals with the development in field of culture have been surrounded by ritual observances.

Folk lores

Folk dance, folk songs and folk music play vital role in the cultural life of the Gonds. It is through music and dance that they keep themselves occupied in the evenings. Folk music and dance give expression to their innermost feelings, their joys and sorrows, their nat ıral affections and ideals, their appreciation of beauty of nature and war.

Every season and every socio-religious ceremony has specific songs. On the occasions of their important religious festivals and marriages, they are found dancing and singing whole day and night. Both the sexes take active part in singing and dancing.

Folk dance of Gonds are popularly called as '*Karma*'. 'Karma' is the name of the plant commonly grown in that area- Before beginning the ceremonial dance a stem of the plant called '*Karam Kalla*' is buried in the ground and the dancing-troupe dance around this plant. Another interpretation of '*Karma*' given by the local inhabitants, refer to the symbolic meaning attached to 'kar' which means hand and 'ma' means to me. Thus, *Karma* is to "give your hand to me and dance", as the movements in the dance involve holding of hands. This interpretation of *Karma* appears quite logical.

Festivals

The festivals of Gonds are not so much associated with religion as is the case with most Hindu festivals. Their festivals are in response to the harvest season and local customs. Due to their frequent contact with Hindu population, their folk-ways are now becoming apparently tinged with the colour of Hinduism. Gonds observe may Hindu festivals without understanding their religious significance. Most celebrations consist of offerings to gods, feasts drinking and dancing. On the whole, their festivals tend to be recreational rather than spiritual. Their festivals are also connected with agricultural cycle. Their enthusiasm and zeal depends upon the success of harvest. Festivals are the only occasions in which Gonds ever indulge in any extravagance, otherwise they believe only in securing two square meals.

Throughout the year a number of fairs, festivals and feasts are organised in the village. However, their distribution over a year is rather irregular.

Hareli: Hareli is the festi al of rain. It is observed in the early period of rains. The goddess of crop 'Kutki Dai' is worshipped on this occasion to ensure better harvest. This is mostly in the month of July-August. 'Hareli' word is probably derived from Hindi word, 'Haryali' which means greenery as in this season vegetation begins to bloom and their is greenery all around.

Khyania: In the month of August seven days before 'Rakhi; Gonds sow the wheat grains in the *Tukania* (Basket). On the next day of Rakhi i.e. after 8 days they cut the wheat crop from the basket. They exchange this with one another. Some of it is also immersed in the water of Narbada river on the same day. Gonds estimate the success or failure of crop of coming season by this festival.

Rakhi: On the day of Rakhi Gond women imitating the Hindu customs, tie string around the wrist of their brothers and cousins for their safety, security and protection.

Dashera: It is observed in the month of October and is quite an important festival among inmates of Gond villages. But unlike a Hindu festival, it is not associated with any Hindu rites or religious beliefs. Its importance is mainly due to the agricultural ceremony attached to it. During this month the spells of rain ends and active agriculturalseason sets in in the villages. Parties exchange visits and organise dance performances on reciprocal basis. In the hope of getting good crop, Gonds indulge in heavy drinking, throw feasts. *Saila* and *Reena* dances are the common features of the festivals.

Mela Madai: It is held after the completion of the harvesting of the paddy crop, when the people are free from their agricultural work and their stores are full with grain. After Diwali this fair is enjoyed daily for a week. The head of the village inaugrates the Mela. People light oil lamps at their houses. They dance and sing day and night. This celebration is made in the happiness of the success of their harvest. Sweet dishes and special food items are prepared in Gond houses on this occasion.

Chait Gal: This festival starts from 'Sharad Purnima' after Dashera (October) and continues upto the 'Kartic Purnima' of Diwali (November). Gonds stand in the open ground along a wooden pole smeared with grease. On the top of the pole is tied a cloth in which a coconut, some currency and sweets are wrapped. Skilled and courageous unmarried boys try to climb on the pole to get the things tied on the top of the pole. Unmarried girls and other villagers make efforts, so that a person does not succeed climbing up and get at the things. The moment an ambitious youth starts climbing the pole the girls around the pole starts beating him with sticks. When he gets down with the things, his friends grab him and run away.

On the last day in midnight of 'Kartik Purnima' the unmarried boys take bath in the nullah.

Nawa Feast: In this festival, harvest thanking is celebrated. New harvested rice is offered to 'Bara Dev' under a Saj Tree for the first time new rice is cooked in the house, by the head of the family who has to keep fast on that day. On this occasion women folk do not cook rice.

Bidri Ceremony: It starts before the beginning of the sowing of summer crops. It is celebrated to ensure better crop. The 'Gunia' (priest) collect some of the seeds of crops of Kodo, Kutki and other summer grains. He mixes the grains together and sow a little beneath the tree where 'Thakur Dev' lives. He returns little to each cultivator or sows in the centre of the land on which crops are to be grown or mixes it with the whole lot of seed grains to be sown. A feast is given to all those who took part in the Bidri ceremony.

Shankar Chauth: It is eleberated in the months of January and February. Bara Dev festival and Mag Panchami festival are celebrated in July and August respectively.

Holi: It is a spring festival. In the month of March, Holi is celebrated. It is a five day festival. A Gond will never miss the opportunity of drinking alcohol during Holi. On the first day of Holi festival they play with '*Kechar*' (wet soil); on the second day, with Gobar (cow dung) and on the other days with colours. Holi Mela is also held during these days. It is merely a social recreation for Gonds which they have adopted from the local Hindu people.

4

Siz, Distribution and Characteristics of Gond Population

DEMOGRAPHIC analysis begins by ascertaining how many people are there in the area for study and what are the characteristics or the composition of population. According to Hawley (1959), composition refers to the distribution of one or more individually carried traits or attributes. These individual characteristics to which composition generally refers include sex composition, age composition, marital status, education and such other features.

(i) Composition data make possible an elaboration of the description of population;

(ii) These also constitute an inventory of the human resources of a society;

(iii) The data describe the variables essential for analysing demographic processes, such as, birth, death, migration etc. and

(iv) Demographic variables together with population size are important conditions effecting the formation and change of social structure.

Every community has a specified type of composition. The composition of population in most communities is static. It relates to a particular quality of population. The differences in the quality are important to understand the characteristics of the concerned communities.

Each institution of a society pre-supposes a certain number and type of population for the performance of specialised roles or activities that analysis of population composition affords a natural starting point for many kinds of population studies. This is also implied in Hawely's (1959) observation when he opines that "population composition constitutes framework on which rests the institutional structure of the whole society". Various composition elements treated in this chapter are age, sex, marital status, education and occupation.

SEX AND AGE COMPOSITION

Sex and age are both biological factors. Being biological they are independent variables which are necessary for almost all classifications related to population characteristics. Sex and age structure of a population defines the limits of a society's reproductive potential. This structure is also the basic demographic determinant of a country's manpower reserve.

The sex and age structure of a population at any given time is the outcome of its trends in fertility, mortality and territorial movement in the past. It, in turn, influences contemporary levels of birth and death rates and the rate of future population growth.

Sex Composition

Communities differ in sex composition i.e. composition of male and female. It is of fundamental importance, both demographically and socially. Sex composition affects directly birth rate, death rate and marriage, it appears as a differential in marital status, occupational distribution.

In any given area the distribution of sexes tends to be unequal owing to the operation of any of the three factors :

—A differential sex-ratio at birth is universal. More males are born everywhere than females.

—At all ages, death rate of males is usually higher than those of females.

—Migration is sex-selective. In long distance movements, males tend to outnumber females, but in short distance movements females usually pre-dominate.

Sex ratio can be calculated as number of females per thousand males.

$$\text{Sex ratio} = \frac{\text{Number of females}}{\text{Number of males}} \times 1000$$

Since 1901 sex ratio in India has been subjected to continuus depletion except a minor exception in 1951. The sex ratio in Madhya Pradesh has been higher than all India average, but it has also suffered a decline, much in line with the position in the country since 1901 to 1934. The sex-ratio in India and Madhya Pradesh during different census years was as under:

Table 4.1

Distribution of Sex ratio in India and Madhya Pradesh

Census year	India	Madhya Pradesh
1901	972	990
1911	963	986
1921	953	974
1931	940	973
1941	934	970
1951	947	967
1961	941	953
1971	930	941
1981	933	941

(Source: After M.K. Premiet al, 1983).

Table 4.2

Distribution of Households and Sex-wise Population of Gonds

Clan group	Number of households	Total population	Number of males	Number of females	Sex ratio F/M x 1000	
Maravi	20	124	62	62	1000	
Oikey	6	41	19	22	1158	A
Partai	10	63	32	31	969	
Wayam	10	10	5	5	1000	
Warkara	15	97	53	44	830	
Chai-devki	2	11	6	5	833	
Neti	7	46	25	21	840	B
Sariyam	1	17	9	8	889	
Sat-devki	2	13	7	6	857	
Sirsam	1	9	5	4	800	
Kurwati	1	10	6	4	667	
Kushram	2	22	14	8	571	C
Dhumkati	1	11	4	7	1750	
	78	474	247	227	919	

Sex Ratio among Tribals

Unlike the position in India, Madhya Pradesh tribal population has had the privilege of having favourable sex ratio (higher number of females than males). According to 1961 census, the sex ratio among the tribes of Madhya Pradesh was 1003 females per 1000 males. But this lead could not be maintained in 1971 consus and the sex-ratio also declined to 998.

Table 4.2 gives the clan-wise sex ratio of the village population. The table shows that the sex ratio of the village is 919. The sex ratios of the village are divided ratio three groups :

Group A—showing the sex ratios approximately at par with males. (i.e. 1000).

Group B—showing moderately lower sex ratio (i.e. 800-900).

Group C—showing highly low sex ratio (i.e. 500-600).

The clan *Dhumkati*, has a sex ratio of 1750 which is much higher than normal. This group is not included above because the number of households is only one which is very low to prove anything.

Table 4.3 gives the clan-wise distribution of sex-ratios in various age groups.

Age Composition

The age structure of population is the basic concept of population composition. Almost every aspect of human behaviour, physical capability, mental maturity and attitudes objective characteristics vary with the age attained. It has got bearing on the role and functioning of the society. The extensive change in age composition result in adaptive changes in many areas of its behaviour. Its influence is more conspicuous in the composition of labour force. Thus, the age composition of the population constitutes the framework, on which the institutional structure of the entire society rests.

In a demographic study of age composition an analysis of the proportion of the total population in each stage of life

Table 4.3

Clan-wise Distribution of Sex-Ratio

Clan-group	General Sex-ratio	Age-Groups 0-4	5-9	10-14	15-19	20-24	25-29	30-34	35-39	40-44	45-49	50-54	55-59	60+
Maravi	1000	750	500	1222	1667	2333	1000	1500	429	600	400	1000	333	2000
Warkara	764	800	455	500	571	1500	2000	1500	10. 0	500	1500	500	—	—
Partai	909	1750	2333	333	750	667	2000	1000	250	—	—	—	—	500
Oikey	1158	333	667	1250	—	3000	1000	—	1000	—	1000	—	—	—
Neti	769	333	1667	1500	500	2000	1000	—	—	333	—	—	—	—
Sariyam	625	500	1000	—	—	1000	1000	—	—	—	—	—	—	—
Sirsam	800	1000	1000	—	—	—	—	—	—	—	—	—	—	—
Sat-devki	625	—	—	500	500	—	—	—	—	—	—	—	—	—
Kurwati	667	—	—	—	500	1000	—	—	—	—	—	—	—	—
Kushram	467	—	667	—	1000	500	—	—	—	—	—	—	—	—
Dhumkati	1750	—	—	—	—	1000	—	—	—	—	—	—	—	—
Wayam	1000	—	1000	1000	—	—	1000	—	—	—	—	—	—	—
Chai-devki	833	—	—	—	1000	—	—	500	—	—	—	—	—	—

cycle, changes therein, regional variation and factors affecting such variations are involved. Age shares the universal recognition accorded to sex. It is important demographically and socially in composition of population. The roles and responsibilities of a society are distributed according to the age attained by an individual.

The age composition of a population is a product of the birth, death and migration rates. It is biologically related to fertility and mortality. Birth rates and death rates can meaningfully be compared and interpreted only when age and sex composition of population is taken into consideration. In non-literate areas individuals often do not remember their correct date/year of birth. Thus data on age is less reliable than sex data. There is a tendency of respondents to concentrate on the numbers ending with zero and five.

Keeping in view the importance of all characteristics of population, population of the village has been analysed by age and sex.

Table 4.4 shows the population distribution of the village by age and sex. The maximum population density is indicated in the age-group of 0-4 years and sex ratio of the group is 789.5. The age group 15-49 comprises total population 287 (60.4%) out of which 145 are males and 142 females. This age group is considered most significant in terms of fertility. The economically active group i.e. 15-59 year consists of 278 persons (58.6%) out of which 142 are males and 136 females. Economically inactive group i.e. 0-15 and 60 consists of 195 persons (43.2%).

Dependency Ratio

The dependency ratio is defined as :

$$\text{Dependency ratio} = \frac{\text{Population under 15 years} + \text{Population 60 years and over}}{\text{Population aged 15-59 years}} \times 100$$

Table 4.4

Distribution of Population by Age and Sex

Age Group	Total Population		Males		Females		
	Number	%	Number	%	Number	%	Sex ratio= F/Mx1000
0-4	68	14.3	38	15.4	30	13.2	789
5-9	62	13.1	34	13.8	28	12.3	824
10-14	57	12.0	30	12.1	27	11.9	900
15-19	52	11.0	22	8.9	30	13.2	1364
20-24	41	8.7	17	6.9	24	10.6	1412
25-29	44	6.3	19	7.7	25	11.1	1316
30-34	39	8.2	25	10.2	14	6.2	560
35-39	37	7.8	21	8.5	16	7.0	762
40-44	26	5.5	15	6.1	11	4.8	733
45-49	20	4.2	11	4.4	9	4.0	818
50-54	11	2.3	6	2.4	5	2.2	833
55-59	9	1.9	6	2.4	3	1.3	500
60+	8	1.7	3	1.2	5	2.2	1667
Total	474	100	247	100	227	100	

A large percentage of dependent population tends to reduce savings and investments and inhibits the rate of economic and social advancement of a country as large proportion of scarce resources are diverted towards consumption. Also, an increasingly large number of persons continue to enter the working ages swelling the ranks of the unemployed. Further, certain social and economic processes such as family formation and house purchase, job seeking, retirement and savings and migration and mobility are closely related to the age composition of a population.

Table 4.5 gives the dependency ratios of India, Madhya Pradesh Gond population and the dependency ratio of the village investigated.

Table 4.5

Dependency Ratio

Area	Percentage of population in different age groups			Dependency ratio
	0-14	15-59	60+	
General population of India	40.1	54.6	5.3	83.2
General population of Madhya Pradesh	43.70	50.51	5.79	97.98
Gond population of Madhya Pradesh (1961)	41.44	42.09	16.44	137.51
Gond population of Behanga	39.35	58.86	1.68	69.89

(Source : After Premi et al 1983 and Office of Census of India, Mandla).

According to the Table 4.5 the dependency ratio of the village is the least as compared to the Gond population of Madhya-Pradesh, general population of Madhya Pradesh and the population of India.

Size and Growth of Gond Population

Growth of India's population during the 1970's increased from about 548 million in 1971 to 684 million in 1981, adding 136 million persons in just ten years. The 1981 population of India was almost one and a half times the population of the whole of Africa. The growth of population alone during the decade was equivalent to transferring about half the total population of the USSR or the population of North America (Canada and U.S.A.).

The annual growth rate (G.R.) of the population between two-time points is generally calculated by using the following formula :

$$\text{Growth rate (G.R.)} = \frac{\text{Inerease (or decrease) in Population}}{\text{Base population}} \times 100$$

$$\times$$

$$\text{Number of years}$$

Table 4.6 gives an account of the growth of India's population since 1891.

Table 4.6

Population of India and Its Growth: 1891-1981

Year	Total population	Decennial increase during the decade	Decennial growth rate during the decade (per cent)
1	2	3	4
1891	235.9	—	—
1901	238.4	2.4	1.0

1	2	3	4
1911	252.0	13.7	5.7
1921	251.3	—0.8	—0.3
1931	279.0	27.7	11.0
1941	318.7	39.7	14.2
1951	361.1	42.4	13.3
1961	439.2	78.1	21.6
1971	548.2	108.9	24.8
1981	683.8	135.6	24.8

(Source : After M.K. Premi et al 1983).

Population growth in India since 1891 divides itself into three natural parts, the points of division being 1921 and 1951 respectively (Table 4.6). The year 1921 is called the year of 'Great Divide" because it distinguished the earlier period of chequered population growth from a period of moderately increasing growth. The year 1951 marks the beginning of three decades of rapid population growth.

Since 1921 the factors causing a high death rate have been gradually brought under control and between 1921 and 1951 the country witnessed a gradual rise in population growth rates. The decline in death rate became sharper aftei independence in 1947, with the result that the population nearly doubled from an estimated 347.5 million in 1947 to 683.8 million in 1981.

Unlike the general population in the country for which complete data are available since the turn of the current century, data for tribal population, on uniform pattern are not available. This is a major factor which inhibits vivid presentation of trends in tribal population growth.

The figures of tribal population since 1891 are given as under in Table 4.7.

Table 4.7

Tribal Population in India and its Growth : 1891-1971

Census year	Total tribal population (in millions)	Decennial increase during the decade	Decennial growth rate during the decade (per cent)
1891	16.0	—	—
1901	N.A	—	—
1911	N.A	—	—
1921	16.0	—	—
1931	24.0	8.0	+50.00
1941	N.A	—	—
1951	22.0	—	—
1961	29.8	7.8	+35
1971	37.9	8.1	+27.1

(Source : After Jaiswal, 1981)

The Table 4.7 shows that prior to 1921 census the growth of tribal population was indifferent and figures between 1891 and 1921 remained almost identical. Since 1921 there has been constant increase in tribal population and the period between 1951-61 was marked with sudden spurt when a growth rate of 3.25 per cent was registered. However, the rate of growth during 1961-71 has shown deceleration as compared to the preceding decade and does not correspond with the trend of general growth rate in the country. In case of latter the growth rate has shown further acceleration from 2.16 percent in 1961 to 2.48 per cent in 1971 while tribal population growth rate decreased from 3.25 per cent in 1961 to 2.78 per cent in 1971.

The account of tribal population in Madhya Pradesh is available since 1951. The figures of 1951 census are estimated on the basis of revised Scheduled tribes List Modification Order 1956 while the figures for 1961, 1971 and 1981 are based on actual census enumerations. The population figures are given in Table 4.8.

Table 4.8

Tribal Population in Madhya Pradesh : 1951-1981

Census year	Population	Per cent Decadal variation
1951	48,63,580	—
1961	66,78,410	+37.32
1971	83,87,403	+25.59
1981	119,87,031	+42.92

(Source : After Jaiswal 1981 and Census of India 1981, Series 11, M.P.).

The growth rate during the period, 1961-71 when compared with 1951-61 rate of 37.32 per cent shows a deceleration by 11.73 per cent out of 37.32 percent. However, in actual situation the lower growth rate is mostly ascribable to the fact that growth rate for the period 1951-61 was not accurate because of estimation of tribal population for 1951 census. The decline in growth rate of the tribal population during the decade, comes to 5.47 per cent only. Still, the tribal population during 1961-71 exhibits absolute increase but relative decline. During 1971-81, there has been a substantial increase in the tribal population .

MARITAL STATUS AND MARRIAGE

One of the basic functions of a society is to reproduce itself. As human societies differentiate between mating and reproduction through marriage, the institution of marriage has been found to be universal. This has been further reinforced by social and cultural milieu of each society which, in turn, determines the forms as well as the rules of marriage. Some societies enjoin to their people early marriages of their men and women whereas some others prescribe late marriages. Thus, the social structure of different societies have greatly influenced the marriage pattern round the world. Among the Hindus, who form more than 80 per cent of country's population, the primary role of a woman has remained that of a mother and every man is ordained to marry in order that his family is perpetuated through son. Even in other relegious communities like Muslims, Sikhs and Christians the practice of universal marriage is quite prevalent in the country.

Marital status in a population varies significantly with age and sex. In countries where the population has comparatively larger proportion of young population, the proportion of never married persons can be higher provided the age of marriage is not very low. If the population has a comparatively older structure, the proportion of never married persons will be low.

Further, the social structure of different societies have greatly influenced the marriage pattern around the world. For example, we find polygamy among the Muslims which probably creates greater differentials between the average age of the bridegroom and the bride at the time of marriage. Certain customs involve group marriages in some specific communities. In communities where child marriages are still quite prevalent, the proportion of never married is expected to be low.

Marital status as an element of composition is of considerable importance. It has a direct bearing on the computation of measures of reproduction. Differences in marital status have direct bearing on both fertility and mortality. The age at which people get married and the proportion of the populations that actually gets married is an important determinant of the fertility. Since, in general, fertility is higher in places where marriages are concluded early and where the proportions of marriages is high. Mortality also varies with marital status, both married male and married females have lower death rate than unmarried persons of the same age. In part these differentials arise from the fact that marriage is selective or the greater longevity of marriage may result from the better personal care and greater regularity which usually characterise married life.

When viewed comparatively, such data are useful indicators of social, economic and cultural differences among different populations. The information about marital status is generally included by demographers as it has many advantages.

Table 4.9 shows the distribution of village population with respect to marital status. It shows that below 15 years of age only 2 persons are married. There are 192 individuals below 15 years who are unmarried. Out of these 192 individuals, 104 are males while 88 are females. Total married males are 88 while married females are 94. There are 5 widowers and 18 widows in the village.

Age at Marriage

One important aspect of the study of marital status of any given population is to know the average age of the bridegroom and the bride at the time of marriage. This aspect becomes important in human societies because reproduction basically takes place in wedlock. Moreover, in societies where early marriages are prevalent, one finds that, on an average, a woman bears a greater number of children during her childbearing span as compared to those where late marriages (average age of bride being 22 years and above) are prevalent.

Table 4.9

Marital Status of the Gonds of Behanga

Age-group	Married		Unmarried				Divorced	
	Male	Female	Male	Female	Widower	Widow	Male	Female
0-9	—	—	72	58	—	—	—	—
10-14	—	2	32	30	—	—	—	—
15-19	4	8	15	18	—	—	—	—
20-24	9	16	6	4	—	—	—	—
25-29	13	18	4	—	—	1	—	2
30-34	9	11	1	—	—	—	4	8
35-39	16	14	—	—	—	—	3	—
40-44	12	8	—	—	—	1		2
45-49	9	11	—	—	2	4	7	—
50-54	11	4	—	—	—	3	3	—
55-59	2	1	—	—	1	5	—	—
60+	3	1	—	—	2	4	—	—
Total	88	94	130	110	5	18	17	12

Table 4.10

Mean Age at Marriage by Sex in India : 1901-1981 (in years)

Year	Male	Female
1901	20.0	13.1
1911	20.3	13.2
1921	20.7	13.7
1931	18.6	12.7
1941	19.9	14.7
1951	19.9	15.6
1961	21.3	15.5
8971	22.4	17.2
1981	23.3	18.3

(Source: *Child in India*, 1985).

Table 4.10 gives the mean age at marriage by sex in India. In India girls marry early and universally. This pattern is due to "feasibility" and "desirablility" of marriage. "Feasibility" is determined primarily by expectations of financialand residential independence of the couple, including dower of dowry requirements and by the availability of resources. It is obvious that marriage is feasible under the joint family system Indian low conditions of living. "Desirability" is determined by the availability of social and institutional alternatives to marriage, child bearing and by the extent to which these alternatives are considered rewarding. Under this category, we should consider "the penalteis of marrying late or never, in particular the penalties of childlessness, social rotation and stigma, and the loss of opportunities for economic support and social mobility (especially important for women)". The situation prevaling in India on these matters is such that marriage has become universal (Jain, 1975).

Table 4.11

Comparative Account of Mean Age at Marriage of Different Clans of Gond

Clans	Mean age at marriage	
	Male	Female
Maravi	18	16
Warkara	18	16
Oikey	19	15
Neti	19	16
Partai	18	17
Kushram	19	16
Dhumkati	20	16
Sariyam	20	17
Chai-devki	19	15
Sat-devki	19	15
Sirsam	19	16
Kurwati	20	17
Wayam	19	16
Mean age	19	16

Table 4.11 gives a comparative account of mean age at marriage of different clans of Gond in Behanga. The Table shows that the mean age at marriage among girls is 16 years and for boys it is 19 years, which is quite low as compared to the mean age at marriage in India i.e. 18.3 for girls and 23.3 for boys.

OCCUPATIONAL COMPOSITION

The pattern of occupation signifies the general structure of economy, level of living, involvement of persons in different activities. In a predominantly agricultural country, agriculture stands as the mainstay of the economy. The tribal economy is no exception to the rule.

Pattern of occupation is an index of economic status, level of living, involvement of persons in different activities and socio-cultural development. Gonds are far more dependent on agriculture and forestry than any othar segment of the society. But the agricultural conditions among the Gonds are miserably poor. More than 93 per cent of the Gond population was found dependent on agriculture, livestock and forestry, according to the various reports, and remaining population of Gond were dependent on all other activities including household industries. Thus, it becomes evident that the Gonds are heavily dependent on agriculture which is still operated with primitive tools and equipment. *Bewar* (i.e. shifting cultivation) is still practised in certain areas of Durg, Mandla, Bastar Chhindwara, Raigarh and Surgiya district.

Besides, in agriculture Gonds are subject to vagaries of monsoon, the irrigation facilities being almost absent. Heavy intensity of soil erosion, inhospitable terrain etc. keep it below the subsistence level.

It is to be noted that in 1951 census of India the classification of worker and non-worker was based on "income approach" in which persons were classified as "self-supporting", "earning dependents", "non-earning dependents". However, this approach was given up by 1961 cesnus. At this stage a person was considered as 'worker' in such activities like cultivation, dairying, household industry. Any woman in addition to her household work engaged herself in work for sale or wages, or in domestic service for wages for others, was treated as worker.

The 1971 census defined a wroker as follows:A "worker" was a person whose main activity was participation in any economically productive work by his physical or mental activity. Work involved not only actual work but also effective supervision and direction of work.

In the 1981 census information of workers has been collected at 2 levels :

1. Main activity as worker and
2. Whether worked at any time at all during the last year.

Since 1981 the definition of worker has been changed and now the population is divided into:

(i) Main worker;
(ii) Marginal worker; and
(iii) Non-workers.

This is a departure from 1971 census, where the population was divided into worker and non-worker and the former had 9 categories which includes cultivators, agricultural labourers, livestock, forestery, fishing, construction, trade and commerce etc.

Table 4.12

Position of workers and Non-workers in India (1981)

	Workers	Number
1.	Total workers	65.82 crores
2.	Main-workers	22.01 crores
3.	Marginal workers	2.71 crores
4.	Non-workers	41.10 crores

(Source: After Premi et al 1983)

Table 4.13

Occupational Distribution of Clans

Sub—tribes/ Clans	Agriculture	Student	Teacher	Forest Service	Labour	Karyana shop	Non-workers
Maravi	60	21	1	1	2	—	39
Warkara	44	15	1	—	—	—	37
Oikey	17	9	—	—	—	1	14
Neti	25	6	—	—	1	—	14
Partai	29	9	—	—	—	—	25
Kushram	11	6	—	—	1	—	4
Dhumkats	5	3	—	—	—	—	3
Chai-devki	4	4	—	—	1	—	2
Sat-devki	8	5	—	—	—	—	0
Kurwati	7	3	—	—	—	—	0
Sirsam	4	2	—	—	—	—	4
Wayam	3	1	—	—	—	1	5
Serivam	9	3	—	—	—	—	7
Total	226	87	2	1	5	2	154

Table 4.13 shows the classification of workers on the basis of occupation. It is evident from the Table that working population in the village Behanga is 48.78% of the total population while non-working population of the village is 51.22% of the total population. Non-working population consists of 154 individuals. Non-working population includes school going childern, house wives, very old persons and other handicapped people. They are assumed to be non-workers because they do not directly contribute to economy.

The main occupation of the people of the village Behanga is agriculture. Only a few people are involved in other jobs like teaching, forest service, *karyana* shop or are labourers. They in all are 10 out of the total of 474 individuals i.e., only 2.10% individuals. In spite of the fact that the members of this small population are holding secondary jobs there main occupation is still agriculture. Their lands are looked after by other members or the family like wives and children.

Educational Status

In the Indian census a person is regarded as literate if he or she is able to read and write a simple message with understanding in any language. On this basis at the time of the 1981 census, there were 36.23 percent (29.5% in 1971) literate people in the total population of the country. The literacy rate of the population can be calculated by the following formula :

$$\text{Literacy rate} = \frac{\text{Number of literate persons of specified sex and area}}{\text{Population of persons of that sex and area}} \times 100$$

The Table 4.14 gives the picture of literacy rate in India from 1951 to 1981. This Table also indicates that the pace of growth of literacy has been faster in rural areas than in urban areas and faster among females than among males. One of the reason for this pattern lies in the fact that the starting base in rural areas is much lower than that in urban areas and, similarly, much lower in case of females than males.

As a demographic characteristic, educational status is used as an index of well-being, of socio-economic position or in general of the degree of familiarity with culture and the receptivity to new ideas and information on the part of individuals. The importance of education in the modern world is so evident that it needs no exposition. In this sense, educational status has direct relevance for a wide array of concerns, ranging from measurement of fertility, mortality and other demographic events to the inventories of the human resources of societies and the possibility of systematic social change. It is for such reason that educational data are collected by the census agencies in the most nations. In most advanced countries illiteracy has been almost eliminated. Questions on literacy are no longer included in their census.

The educational status of the people is one of the most important cultural variable which influence the reproductive behaviour of the people. The various studies have shown positive relationship between the educational attainments of households and their outlook towards the size of family, age at marriage, attitudes towards use of contraception etc.

According to I.Z. Hussain (1972), there exists :

- a positive relationship between the educational attainment of the household members including its head and the mean age at marriage of males and females,
- a strong negative relationship between fertility and educational status of the household.
- direct relationship of preference of 2 or 3 children with the educational level of head and household member and
- an increase in the proportion of opinion in favour of liberalisation of abortion laws with a rise in educational status.

Table 4.14

Literacy Rates in India by Sex and Rural Urban Residence, 1951-1981

Year	Total			Rural			Urban		
	Male	Female	Total	Male	Female	Total	Male	Female	Total
1951	24.9	7.9	16.6	—	—	—	—	—	—
1961	34.5	13.0	24.0	29.1	8.5	19.0	57.5	34.5	47.0
1971	39.5	18.7	29.5	33.8	13.2	23.7	61.3	42.1	52.4
1981	46.7	24.8	36 1	40.6	18.0	29 6	65.6	47.6	57.2

(Source: After Premi, 1983).

Although the tribal people have little benefit of higher education yet their customs relating to marriage keep the age at marriage comparatively higher and the lack of higher education has not stood as an impediment. The improvement of education among the tribes may, therefore, futher accelerate the process of rise in age at marriage and decline in fertility.

Table 4.15 shows the educational status of the population of village Behanga. It is evident from Table 4.15 that out of 474 persons 368 persons are illiterates. Therefore, it can be said that 77.6% of the total population is illiterate. The educational qualification above matric is nil. There are no graduates or post-graduates in the vallage.

Approximately 4% population of the village can read and write although the percentage of individuals studying from primary upto matric level is 17%. Thus the literacy rate of the entire village is quite low.

Table 4.16 shows that there are total 119 children of age group 5-14 years which are expected to attend schools. But only 45 children go to school. Most of the children go to a primary school of the village. 37.8% of the children of age group 5-14 years are literate.

Table 4.15

Educational Status of Different Gond Literates

Sub-Tribe	Illiterates			Primary			Middle			Matric			Graduate			Read and Write			Total
	M	F	T	M	F	T	M	F	T	M	F	T	M	F	T	M	F	T	
Maravi	33	51	84 (67.7)	11	7	18 (14.5)	7	2	9 (7.2)	3	—	3 (2.4)	—	—	—	8	2	10 (8.0)	124
Warkara	37	40	77 (79.3)	6	2	8 (8.2)	3	1	4 (4.1)	2	—	2 (2.0)	—	—	—	5	1	6 (6.1)	97 (100.00)
Oikey	11	19	30 (73.3)	3	3	6 (14.6)	2	—	2 (4.8)	—	—	1 (2.4)	—	—	—	2	—	2 (9.7)	41 (100.00)
Neti	22	20	42 (91.3)	3	1	4 (8.6)	—	—	—	—	—	—	—	—	—	—	—	—	46 (100.00)
Partai	27	31	58 (92.0)	2	1	3 (4.7)	2	—	2 (3.1)	—	—	—	—	—	—	—	—	—	63 (100.00)
Kushram	8	7	15 (68.1)	2	1	3 (13.6)	3	—	3 (13.6)	—	—	—	—	—	—	1	—	1 (4.5)	22 (100.00)
Dhumkati	3	7	10 (90.9)	—	—	—	1	—	1 (9.0)	—	—	—	—	—	—	—	—	—	11 (100.00)

Chai-Dovki	6	5	11 (100)	—	—	—	—	—	—	—	—	—	—	—	—	—	—	—	11 (100.00)
Sat-devki	3	4	7 (53.8)	5	1	6 (46.1)	—	—	—	—	—	—	—	—	—	—	—	—	13 (100.00)
Kurwati	6	4	10 (100)	—	—	—	—	—	—	—	—	—	—	—	—	—	—	—	10 (100.00)
Srisam	3	4	7 (77.1)	1	—	1 (11.1)	1	—	1 (11.1)	—	—	—	—	—	—	—	—	—	9 (100.00)
Wayam	3	5	8 (80.0)	1	—	1 (10.0)	—	—	—	—	—	—	—	—	—	—	—	—	10 (100.00)
Sariyam	4	5	9 (69.2)	2	—	2 (15.3)	2	—	2 (15.3)	—	—	—	—	—	—	—	—	—	13 (100.00)
Total	166	202	368 (77.6)	36	16	52 (10.9)	21	3	24 (5.0)	5	—	5 (1.05)	—	—	—	16	3	19 (4.0)	474 (100.00)

Table 4.16

Clan-wise Literacy Among Children of Age Group 5-14 Years

Sub-tribe/ Clan	Total number of childern of age-group of 5-14 years			Number of School going childern of 5-14 years			Percentage of School going children
	M	F	T	M	F	T	
Maravi	18	17	35	9	6	15	42.8
Warkara	20	9	29	6	3	9	31.0
Oikey	5	6	11	2	2	4	36.3
Neti	5	7	12	2	—	2	16.6
partai	9	5	14	4	4	8	
Kushram	2	1	3	1	1	2	66.6
Dhumkati	2	—	2	1	—	1	50.0
Chai-devki	2	1	3	—	1	1	33.3

Sat-devki	1	—	1	—	—	—	—
Kurwati	1	—	1	—	—	—	—
Sirsam	2	1	3	—	1	1	33.3
Wayam	—	1	1	—	1	1	100.0
Sariyam	3	1	4	1	—	1	25.0
Total	70	49	119	26	19	45	37.8

5

Demographic Processes

THE population of an area increases by births and decreases by deaths if the area is not affected by immigration and emigration. The difference between the births and deaths is called "natural increase" in the population. Besides, if the area has also gained in population through larger immigration than emigration, this increase is due to migration. However, net emigrating areas lose part of their natural increase (and sometimes, even more than their natural increase) over time if the people largely move out to other areas and very few people, if at all, immigrate.

Rapid population growth as observed in India and most of the developing countries of the world in the second half of this century has been due to a fast decline in mortality and continuation of a high level of fertility.

For the study of population dynamics one should have the following information :

(a) The number of events that occur.

(b) The population to which the events occur.

(c) The interval of time during which the events occur.

As the events of births and deaths occur continuously in a population, they have to be recorded side by side for which vital registration system is established. From the recorded events, it is easy to tabulate events by each week, calendar month or year as they are required.

FERTILITY

Fertility, being one of the most fundamental determinants of population growth, represents an essential feature in our approach to the understanding of human society. Fertility affects, directly or indirectly, every aspect of social and economic life. In underdeveloped countries population explosion (baby boom) has been acting as a constraint to economic development.

In the words of Thompson and Lewis (1965): "Fertility is generally used to indicate the actual reproductive performance of a woman or a group of women. The crude birth rate (number of births per 1000 population per year) is only one measure of fertility".

It is important here to distinguish between the two terms, fertility and fecundity. Fertility and fecundity are two fundamentally distinct entities. Fecundity is a biologieal concept which designates the physiological reproductive potentiality of a species. People lacking the capacity to procreate on account of pathological or physiologieal abnormalities are referred to as 'sterile'. Sterility may be permanent on just a passing phase. On the other hand, fertility refers to the actual occurrence of births and especially live births. Fecundity cannot be measured easily whereas fertility can be measured as the frequency of births in a population in one year.

Physiologically, human females are capable of reproduction roughly between the age 15-49 years. Theoretically a human female can bear 15-20 children.

Table 5.1 gives the average decade birth rates in India, 1901-81. The birth rate in India has long remained at a high level. The sudden slump in the figure for 1941-51 decade is because of the difference in methodology adopted for that decade for estimated age structure which, in turn, affected the estimate of birth rate. The data, however, indicate a clear pattern of declining birth rate in the Indian population.

Table 5.1

Average Decade Birth Rate in India: 1901-1981

Decade	Birth rate
1901-11	49.2
1911-21	48.1
1921-31	46.2
1931-41	45.2
1941-51	39.9
1951-61	41.7
1961-71	41.1
1971-81	33.3

(Source : After Premi et al, 1983)

Table 5.2 gives the average decade birth rates in Madhya Pradesh. The table shows a sickly downward trend in birth rates in Madhya Pradesh. The birth rate during 1951-60 declined to 43.2 from 45.1 in the preceding decade in Madhya Pradesh while in India it registered increase from 39.9 during 1941-50 to 41.7 during 1951-60.

Table 5.2

Average Decade Birth Rate in Madhya Pradesh: 1901-81

Decade	Birth rate
1901-10	47.1
1911-20	45.1
1921-30	41.4
1931-40	41.2
1941-50	45.1
1951-60	43.2
1961-70	40.7
1971-80	38.5

(Source : After Premi et al, 1983 and Child in India, 1985)

Measure of fertility

As the numbers of births in a year in any given population will depend on its size, it is necessary to convert the births into some sort of a rate to make any comparison (over space or over time) feasible. Hence, demographers have evolved a number of measures of fertility. The various rates obtained by making use of vital registration date are known as direct fertility measures while those derived from census statistics alone are known as indirect fertility measures.

There are several methods of finding out fertility rate. These are :

(1) Crude Fertility Rate (CFR)

(2) General Fertility Rate (GFR)

(3) Age Specific Fertility Rate (ASFR)

(4) Gross Fertility Rate (GFR)

In the investigation in question in the village, the total number of female population is 227 out of whieh 99 are mothers i.e., they have borne children and 128 are non-mothers. The total number of children born by 99 mothers are 247.

Table 5.3

Fertility Rate among Respondents in different Age Groups

Age-group	Total Respondents	Non-Mothers	Mothers	Number of Children
15-19	44	38	6	7
29-24	34	17	17	19
25-29	38	20	18	42
30-34	31	19	12	34
35-39	29	15	14	49
40-44	18	9	9	29
45-49	11	2	9	22
50 and above	22	8	14	45
	227	128	99	247

Crude Fertility Rate

Thompson and Lewis (1965) have defined crude fertility rate as "the crude fertility rate for any specified population is obtained by dividing the number of births recorded in that population during a specified year by its total number, which gives a fraction of births per person....This rate is called crude because all differences in composition between populations are ignored in calculating it".

$$\text{Crude Fertility Rate} = \frac{T}{P} \times K$$

(CFR)

T= Total number of live births during the mid-year population

P= Total mid-year population

K= Constant (generally taken as 1000)

Table 5.4

Clan-wise Crude Fertility Rate (CFR)

Clan grop	Total population	Total No. of live births	CFR $\frac{T}{P}$ XK
Maravi	124	4	32.25
Warkara	97	2	20.61
Oikey	41	2	48.78
Kushram	22	1	45.45
Chai-devki	11	1	90.90
Dhumkati	11	—	—
Neti	46	2	43.47
Partai	63	3	47.61
Wayam	10	1	100.00
Sariyam	17	2	117.64
Sat-devki	13	1	76.92
Sirsam	9	—	—
Kurwati	10	1	00.00
Total	474	20	42.19

It is evident from Table 5.4 that there are 42.19 births per 1000 persons in the village. The maximum crude fertility rate is amongst Sariyam and no crude fertility rate is measured in Dhumkati and Sirsam clans.

General Fertility Rate

General fertility rate is a refined method as compared with crude fertility rate. In this method effects of age and sex are taken into account. Thompson and Lewis (1965) defined that the general fertility rate is usually four to five times as high as the crude fertility rate in the same population, because the women of those age normally constitute of one fifth to one fourth of the total population. It can be calculated as:-

$$\text{General Fertility Rate (a)} = \frac{T}{P} \times K$$

(GFR)

T= Total number of live births in mid-year population.

P= Mid-year population of women of reproductive age group i.e. 15-49 years

K= Constant (generally taken as 1000)

According to Table 5.5 the general fertility rate of entire population of the village is 229.88 i.e. 229 births per thousand women in mid-year

Table 5.5

Clan-wise General Fertility Rate

Clan-group	Total female population of reproductive age group	Total No. of live births	$GFR = \frac{T}{P} \times K$
Maravi	28	4	142.85
Warkara	20	2	100.00
Oikey	9	2	222.22
Kushram	1	1	1000
Chai-devki	1	1	1000
Dhumkati	2	—	—

Neti	9	2	222.22
Partai	11	3	272.72
Wayam	1	1	1000
Sariyam	2	2	1000
Sat-devki	1	1	1000
Sirsam	1	—	—
Kurwati	1	1	1000
Total	87	20	229.88

General fertility rate can be calculated in more specifie or refined form. That is by excluding the widows, unmarried girls and divorced women and taking into account only those women who are actually capable of reprodction. It can be calculated by the formula:

General Fertility Fate (b)= $\frac{T'}{P'} \times K$
(GFR)

T'= Total number of live births in mid-year population
P'= Mid-year population of women who are actually capable of reproduction
K= Constant (generally taken as 1000)

Table 5.6

General Fertility Rate (b)

Clan group	Actual reproductive female population	No. of live births	GFR= $\frac{T'}{P'}$ XK
Maravi	21	4	190.47
Warkara	17	2	117.64
Oikey	7	2	285.71
Kushram	1	1	1000
Chai-devki	1	1	1000
Dhumkati	1	—	—
Nati	4	2	500.00
Partai	5	3	600.00
Wayam	1	1	1000
Sariyam	2	2	1000
Sat-devki	1	1	1000
Sirsam	1	—	—
Kurwati	1	1	1000
Total	63	20	317.46

Table 5.6 shows that the general fertility rate recorded is 317.46. It is high in Kushram, Sat-devki, Wayam, Sariyam, Chaidevki and Kurwati clans i.e. 1000. While it is minimum in Oikey clan i.e. 285.71. No child birth is recorded in Dhumkati and Sirsam sub-tribes.

SAge pecific Fertility Rate

It is an important refinement in the measurements of natality without which other refinements in many cases cannot be made. In the words of Thompson and Lewis (1965). "Age specific fertility rates for any year are obtained by dividing the number of births to mothers or each age in that year by the number of women of this age in population at that date and multiplying the figure by 1000. Age specific birth rate is the number of births per 1000 women of a given age per year". Such a rate ean be found out with the help of following formula:

$$\text{Age Specific Fertility Rate} = \frac{b_1}{p_1} \times K.$$

(ASFR)

b_1= No. of live births to the mother of specified age-group in mid-year population

p_1= Mid-year population of mothers of that specified age-group

K= Constant (generally taken as 1000)

This measure is preferred over others because in this method, it is accepted that all women in all groups do not have the same reproductive capacity change with age. It is possible to study the actual cohort of women, whether the reproductive capacity of women has decreased or increased.

Table 5.7

Age Specific Fertility Rate

Age-group	Mothers of specified age group	No. of live births to the mothers of that specific age group.	$ASFR=\frac{b_i}{p_i}\times K$
15-19	6	3	500.00
20-24	17	5	294.11
25-29	18	8	444.44
30-34	12	2	166.66
35-39	14	2	142.85
40-44	9	—	—
45-49	9	—	—
Total	85	20	235.29

Table 5.7 indicates the rate of birth per thousand mother in different age-groups. No births have been recorded in the age groups 40-44 and 45-49. The highest age specific fertility rate in specified age group is 15-19 i.e. 500.00. This indicates that the women in this age group are most fertile.

Gross Fertility Rate

In order to calculate gross fertility rate, we take into account only the mothers of specified age group excluding the women incapable of reproduction, widows and unmarried girls etc. and the female child born to the mothers of that specified age group in mid-year population. The female children are the future mothers. We assume that all will live through the child bearing age i.e. 15-49 years and that age-specific birth rate prevailing will continue throughout the child bearing life of the group of women under consideration.

Gross Fertility Rate $= \frac{Bf}{M} \times K$
(GFR)

Bf = No. of female children born to mothers of specific age group

M = Total no. of mothers of that specific age group

K = Constant (generally taken as 1000)

Table 5.8

Gross Fertility Rate

Age group	Total No. of mothers of specific age-group	No. of female children born to mothers of that specific age group	GFR $= \frac{Bf}{M} \times K$
15-19	6	1	166.66
20-24	17	2	117.64
25-29	18	4	222.22
30-34	12	1	83.33
35-39	14	—	—
40-44	9	—	—
45-49	9	—	—
Total	85	8	94.11

Table 5.8 indicates that gross fertility rate is the highest in the age group 25-29 years i.e. 222.22. No births are recorded in age groups 35-39, 40-44 and 45-49 years.

This method has its own inherent demerits as it relies on the assumption that fertility as well as death rate are stable and will not change. But in actual practice that is not so.

Determinants of fertility

1) Fertility is very much affected by changes in age at marriage, in the proportions of women married at a

given time and in the spacing of births. Marriage at late age leads to lower fertility whereas marriage at early age leads to higher fertility.

2) Economic status of the people influences fertility. Poverty with its associated factors, such as illiteracy, ill health, poor diet etc. keep the birth rate high. When proportion of protein is lower in the diet, the liver becomes weak, and as a result the oestrogens of the wives cannot be neutralised by the husbands (when the husbands have weak livers). This leads to higher reproductive power among the women. Poverty limits the alternative arrangement for recreation and enjoyment. Prof. De Castro, in his book, *Geography of Hunger*, has pointed out that there is a close relation between poverty and high fertility. Economic prosperity is associated with lower fertility.

3) Religious and social attitudes are important factors determining fertility rate. In traditional societies, there is a preference for large families. Marriage in such societies is a religious duty. Rig Veda says that married woman should bear at least two children. In a society where religious dogmas do not prevail birth rate is generally lower. Where people are tradition oriented birth rate is generally high.

4) Illiteracy and ignorance are responsible for high rate of fertility.

5) Climate is an important factor effecting fertility. The countries having hot climate have higher fertility. The opposite happens in cold climates where the rate of fertility becomes lower.

6) Death rate indirectly affects fertility. Where death rate is high, birth rate has to be high, on the other hand, where death rate is low birth rate may be possibly low.

7) Standard of living influences fertility to a great extent. The desire for higher standard of living will reduce birth rate because the maintenance and education of children will mean extra cost. Higher standard of living leads to lower fertility and lower standard of living leads to higher fertility.

8) Attitudes towards family planning and birth control are equally important factors affecting fertility.

9) Family organisation affects the fertility rate. The joint family system assures joint responsibility of maintaining the children. Therefore, fertility is not restricted. While in a nuclear family this is not possible and thus the fertility rate is minimised.

10) Social customs and traditions influence fertility to a great extent. For exmple, in a society where widow remarriage system is prevalent, the rate of fertility would be higher.

11) Sterility in women or in men is responsible for lower fertility. The lower the proportion of sterility, the higher is the rate of fertility. Fertility also depends on the physiological capacity to reproduce. The physiological capacity would be higher in case of people of better health and vigour and lower in case of diseased people and people of ill health.

Socio-Economic Factors Responsible for high fertility rate in the Village

1) The primary factor responsible for high fertility rate is the prevalent agricultural system of economy in the village.Under this system, it is believed that every person who works in the field is fully employed and there is no question of his getting employed elsewhere. It is therefore felt that there is tendency to get a boy married at an early age i.e. around 18-20 years.

2) The percentage of illiteracy is very high i.e. more than 85% of the population is illiterate.

3) Poverty is another important factor for high feitility. Sex is the only source for recreation and entertainment. Hence, the fertility rate is very high.

4) The girls are married at a comparatively young age. When the girls are married at a young age, obviously they are exposed to a lengthy period of married life and thus fertility increases.

5) The village exhibits a general trend of widow remarriage. Therefore, when widows remarry they behr children and consequently fertility rate goes up.

6) The children in this village are considered as gifts of God. Hence, social customs are also responsible for high fertility.

7) Most of the people in the village are not aware of family planning and those who are do not practise it. The government has not been in a position to make the people of rural areas realise the need and impoitance of family planning.

FAMILY WELFARE

Family planning or welfare is a constituent of population policy. Family planning is planning of the family, by the family and for the family. By family planning or planned parenthood is meant conscious family limitation or spacing of children by choice and not by chance. It requires the adoption of some suitable methods of birth control.

India is the first country to recognise officially the importance of family planning movement. In India family planning programme was adopted in 1952, but the need of attaching more importance to this programme was stressed during fourth five year plan. It had following objectives :

1) Birth rate would be brought down from 39 per thousand in 1969 to 25 per thousand by 1980-81.

2) Social acceptability of small family.

3) Increasing personal knowledge about family planning devices.

4) Making available the necessary devices and equipment for family planning. In spite of many family welfare programmes and social welfare schemes, birth rate is still very high in India.

Most of the population in India is rural population. In this village the age at marriage is low, economic conditions are poor and backward and faith in customs and traditions are deep rooted. The industrialisation in this region has been fragmentary and scanty. Above all, the death rates, including infant mortality, is higher than the all-India average. The high rate of mortality has been associated with high rate of fertility. Large number of births were there among those families where the rate of survival was low.

The economic base of the state is agriculture, operated still with primitive tools and equipments. Modernisation in agriculture on a large scale is inconceivable in near future The level of living of the rural masses is still poor and, therefore, the decline in fertility through induced efforts has not taken place.

One of the most important and deliberate attempts made to curb the fertility trends, in the village Behanga is through the family planning programmes. The scheme of sterilisation operations, IUD insertions and use of conventional contraceptives are the major instruments in vogue for reducing fertility.

Table 5.9

Family Planning

Age group	Sterilisation operation	Contraceptive devices	Herbal Medicines
25-30	4	3	—
30-35	5	4	—
35-40	6	—	2
40-45	5	—	—
Total	20	7	2

Table 5.9 shows that out of a total of 69 households, 29 families are fallowing family planning programmes i.e. 42% of the total population investigated.

Family planning programmes are for the welfare of human beings. So family planning facilities should be made easily available. People should be educated about family planning programmes to understand its need and significance. They should be motivated to the extent that they opt for family planning.

There are few major factors which do not let the people accept the family planning programme in the village Behanga.

1) Religious attitudes of people. It is believed that any attempt to check reproduction is a sin and against the wish of God. So no serious efforts are made to check child births in the village.

2) Agricultural system of economy. Under this system more people are needed to work in the fields so producing more children is not considered bad by them.

3) Illiteracy and ignorance of people. In the village more than 77% of the population is still illiterate and they do not know the importance and need of family planning.

4) High death rate : As we know that high death rate is associated with high fertility. So, this is one of the very important reasons for not adopting family planning programmes.

The survey of the village reveals that the people are quite aware of the family planning programmes though the application is restricted to a limited number of the couples. People express their desire of having fewer children, but the lack of education and general notion that children are the product of God become impediments in the effectiveness and acceptance of family planning programmes.

MORTALITY

Human beings are mortal. They have to die at some age or the other. Death means permanent extinction of all signs of life from a human body after a birth has taken place. The process of death keeps the population of a given area in some sort of a balance. This happens even when population may be growing in numbers. If it were not there, human race would have swarmed the whole world long ago. Further, mortality patterns and mortality rates provide an index to the state of health of the people.

Mortality or death rate is considered to be a very important demographic process since it effects the population structure. Mortality or death rate is computed by relating the total number of deaths in a given population (excluding still births) during certain period of time, usually a calendar year, to the average number of people living in that population during that period. The death rate is usually expressed as the number of deaths per thousand persons in the population.

Mortality is one of the fundamental factor in determining the size of human population. Population increases the number by addition of births and immigrants, and decreases in the number by deaths and emigration. It influences not only the total size of population but also its composition by sex, age, nativity and race. It is to be taken as the index of well being of the nation.

The interest in mortality, however, embraces more than a study of how mortality affects population change, it also includes the question of why mortality acts as it does. The explanation of the order of dying out of a generation is the concern of demography, medicine and public health, whereas, the latter two disciplines, deal with causes and prevention of deaths. The decline in mortality has been a spectacular as that in fertility but its course seems to have been a different one.

Table 5.10

Estimated Annual Death Rates in India: 1881-1981

Year	Death per thousand population
1881-1891	41.3
1891-1901	44.4
1901-1911	42.6
1911-1921	48.6
1921-1931	36.3
1931-1941	31.2
1941-1951	27.4
1951-1961	22.8
1961-1971	18.8
1971-1981	12.5

(Source : After Premi, 1983 and Child in India, 1985)

Trend in the death rates in India from 1881 onwards is given in Table 5.10. It shows that death rate in India up to 1921 was very high which was due to famine and epidemics. The development of a better communication system after 1921 to carry food from one part of the country to another and more organised efforts to control epidemics like small pox, cholera, and plague helped in bringing the crude death rate down in India from 1921 onwards.

Table 5.11

Estimated Annual Death Rates, Madhya Pradesh: 1901-1981

Year	Death per thousand population
1901-10	33.9
1911-20	45.2
1921-30	31.8
1931-40	31.9
1941-50	38.5
1951-60	23.2
1961-70	17.5
1971-80	12.5

(Source : After Jaiswal, 1979 and Child in India, 1985)

Table 5.11 shows that decline in death rates has been very steady and fast. Madhya Pradesh registered a steep decline in death rate from 38.5 in 1941-50 to 23.2 in 1951-60 as compared to the respective figures of 27.4 and 22.8 in India.

Measures of mortality

Public health authorities, planners and demographers are always interested in knowing the present rates of mortality of population as also other allied details. They are profoundly interested in estimating the likely trend in future also. The mortality rates are, however, measured to find out the pressure of death on population. Some of the methods of finding out death rates are :

1) Crude Death Rate (CDR)

2) Age Specific Death Rate (ASDR)

Crude Death Rate (CDR)

A crude death rate is one which relates the events of death taking place within one year to the mid-year population, without any refinement or standardisation. Assuming linear growth or decline,the population at mid-year is also the average population for the year, and crude birth and death rates measure the frequency of the events to the 'person-year' tried during the year by population at risk. The expression for crude death rate is :

$$CDR = \frac{D}{P} \times K$$

D = Number of deaths in a calendar year

P = Total mid-year population

K = Constant (generally taken as 1000)

The crude rate is widely understood, easy to calculate if the number of events are known, and quite useful as an indicator. Because populations vary substantially in their age and sex compositions, it can only be used for comparative purposes with some precaution.

Table 5.12

Clan-wise Crude Death Rate

Clan-Group	Total population	Number of deaths	Crude Death Rate (CDR)
Maravi	124	5	40.32
Warkara	97	2	20.61
Oikey	41	2	48.78
Kushram	22	1	45.45
Chai-devki	11	—	—
Dhumkati	11	—	—
Neti	46	2	43.47
Partai	63	3	47.61
Wayam	10	—	—
Sariyam	17	2	117.64
Sat-devki	13	1	76.92
Sirsam	9	—	—
Kurwati	10	1	100.00
Total	474	19	40.08

Table 5.12 shows that the crude death rate of the village is 40.08. The maximum crude death rate is recoıded in the clan group Sariyam and no crude death rates are recorded in clan groups Sirsam, Wayam, Chai-devki and Dhumkati.

Age Specific Death Rate

Age specific death rates are refined rates. They are a type of the differential rates. Differential death rates can be calculated in a manner which distinguish the Characteristics for example, ethnicity, socio-economic status or occupation. Age specific death rate can be calculated by :

$$ASDR = \frac{D'}{P'} \times K$$

D′ = Number of deaths in a specific age group

P′ = Total mid-year population

K = Constant (generally taken as 1000)

Table 5.13

Age Specific Death Rate

Age-group	Total population	Number of deaths	ASDR
0-10	130	10	76.92
11-20	109	3	27.52
21-30	85	1	11.76
31-40	76	—	—
41-50	46	2	43.47
50 above	28	3	107.14
Total	474	19	40.08

According to the Table 5.13 the age-specific death rate of the village is 40.08. Maximum age specific death rate is recorded in age-group of 50 and above while no age specific death rate is recorded in age group 21-30 years.

Causes of Mortality

There is always one prime cause that leads to death. The 'cause' can be taken as medical term, denoting the physical character of the abnormality found in the body which lead to death. One cause may lead to another.

Table 5.14 shows the percentage distribution of deaths by major cause group in rural India.

The idea of Gonds about deaths are linked with the theory of disease they believe. Diseases are attributed to the cause of hostile spirits, the ghosts of the dead or breach of some taboos, sorcery and soul loss. The operation of witchcraft is assumed for any untoward accident for which there is no natural explanation. If a child dies, if a tree withers and dries up, if there is an accident, if a cow or bull falls sick, they blame a witch. A woman dying in pregnancy is said to become a witch. Such causes lead them to believe in the treatment of ailment by magicians, like *Gunia* (the spiritist). They believe that what is caused spiritually can be cured spiritually alone. This is one of the factors which stop them from utilising the modern system of medicines.

Table 5.14

Percentage Distribution of Deaths by Major Cause Group in Rural India, 1975—1979

Major cause group (prominent symptoms)	1975	1976	1977	1978	1979
Accidents and injuries	4.6	5.1	4.3	4.9	4.6
Child birth and pregnancy (maternal)	1.0	1.1	1.1	1.0	1.1
Fever	13.2	12.0	10.7	9.6	8.9
Digestive disorders	9.8	9.2	10.6	9.3	9.7
Coughs (disorders of respiratory system)	21.1	20.9	20.6	20.6	20.3
Disorders of central nervous system	3.2	3.6	3.6	3.6	3.6
Diseases of circulatory system	7.0	8.5	8.1	9.0	9.3
Other clear symptoms	7.4	8.2	7.5	7.8	8.3
Causes peculiar to infancy	12.5	12.5	13.2	13.0	13.5
Senility	16.8	17.0	18.3	19.2	18.5
Rest	3.4	1.9	2.0	2.0	2.2
All causes	100.0	100.0	100.0	100.0	100.0

(Source : Population of India, country monograph series No—10; 1982).

INFANT MORTALITY

Infants are easily prone to death and infant mortality is a grave problem in less developed countries and in economically backward communities. Poor people have the highest risk of infant mortality for the obvious reasons of their inability to judge the gravity of the problem (they even hesitate to get their children protected against various diseases like tetanus, whooping-cough, diptheria, small-pox, cholera or polio) and to be able to spare money for treatment.

Two broad groups of deaths to children, under one year, can be distinguished: on the one hand, those that result from causes that precede birth (malformation, debility) or from delivery itself (obstetrical trauma); and on the other, those that can be attributed to the outside enviornment and are caused by lack of hygiene, poor nutrition, infection or accident. The first group of deaths is owing to facts which are called endogenous, the second as exogenous.

For demographic purpose, we consider all children under one year of age as 'infants' and so the term 'infant mortality' refers to mortality among children of less than one year of age. The deaths which occur within a period of 4 months from birth of a child are known as neonatal deaths, whereas those deaths which take place between a period of 4-12 months are known as post-neonatal period deaths.

The infant mortality rate mry be defined as the number of infant deaths that occur per thousand live births in any population in one calendar year. Thus, it is clear that the infant mortality rate does not take into account either foetal death or still births, but only live births and infant deaths.

Live births : Live birth is a complete expulsion or extraction from its mother of a product of conception, irrespective of the duration of pregnaney, which after such separation, breathes or shows any other evidence of life, such as beating of heart, pulsation of the umbilical cord or definite movement of voluntary muscles, whether or not the umbilical cord has been cut or the placenta is attached, each product of such a birth is considered live born.

Foetal death : It is death prior to the complete expulsion or extraction from its mother of a product of conception, irrespective of the duration of pregnancy, the death is indicated by the fact that after such separation the foetus does not breathe or show any other evidence of life such as beating of heart, pulsation of the umbilical cord or definite movement of voluntary muscles.

Infant mortality rate can be measured by the following formula :

$$\text{Infant mortality} = \frac{\text{No. of infant deaths}}{\text{Total no. of live births in mid-year population}} \times 1000$$

Table 5.15

Infant Mortality Rates in India : 1911—1971

Period	Infant mortality	
1911-15	204	(5 years average)
1916-20	219	(„)
1921-25	174	(„)
1926-30	178	(„)
1931-35	174	(„)
1936-40	161	(„)
1941-45	161	(„)
1946-50	134	(„)
1951-1961	146	(Actuarial report)
1961-1971	129	(„)

(Source : Child in India, 1985)

Table 5.15 gives the infant mortality rates in India. It shows that there is a steep fall in infant mortality rate from 1911 to 1971.

Table 5.16

Infant Mortality Rate in Madhya Pradesh

Year	Infant Mortality rate
1941	275.28
1945	256.68
1950	196.07
1960	175.00
1970	94.64

(Source : After Jaiswal, 1983)

Table 5.16 gives the infant mortality rates in Madhya Pradesh. The infant mortality rate, in particular, has always been higher in Madhya Pradesh as compared to other States in India.

Table 5.17

Infant Mortality Rate of Gonds

Age-group	Live-births	Infant deaths	Infant mortality rate
0-7 days	7	2	285.8
7 days—6 months	11	3	272.8
6 months—1year	15	3	200.0

It is clear from the table 5.17 that the infant mortality rate in the village is quite high i.e. 242 per 1000 births.

Causes of Infant mortality among Gonds

The reasons for comparatively higher infant mortality in Gonds are poor economic conditions, discriminating care to female children, lower number of institutional deliveries, high incidence of improvident maternities etc. It is almost a truism that poor class wives have more children than wives in higher income groups. Mothers with large number of children can provide only rationed care.

The economic condition of Gonds is poor, the method of treatment of diseases is primitive and dogmatic, level of literacy is very low, and a larger number of children is considered to be an asset, for they provide additional hands for earning and above all, modern medical facilities and their attendance are scarce. The infant mortality rate in such cases is bound to be high.

MIGRATION

Migration is shifting the home, and not the house. It keeps a balance between the distribution of population and the supply of natural resources. Prof. Hawley has remarked that civilised people are those people who obtained the high degree of mobility. Migration increases mobility.

In the context of migration, we come across two processes 'emigration' and 'immigration'. Emigration refers to going out of a country, while immigration refers to coming in a country. Thus, emigration reduces population of a country while immigration increases it.

Migration can chiefly be of two types:

i) International migration.

ii) Internal migration.

International migration is the migration from one political boundary to another political boundary. It is subject laws regarding migration of the two counties.

Internal migration is the migration from one place to another within the same country. Internal migration may further be of following types:

a) Migration from village to city;

b) Migration from one village to another village;

c) Migration from one city to another; and

d) Migration from city to village;

Motives and factors encouraging migration: Migration, may it be of any sort, is attributable to various factors and is not without certain motives.

The economic motive is the dominant motive for migration. People migrate to places in search of better living. The search for better economic opportunities has been the dominant motive both among international migrants and internal migrants.

There are two factors in migration—the pull factors and the push factors. When people are attracted by the advantages of the new place, the benefits are regarded as pull factors. But when people want to save themselves from the restrictions and disadvantages of the existing place of living, the factors are called the push factors.

Some of the Pull factors are :

a) Attraction towards land: People generally migrate from a place to another where there is much less population on land.

b) Better employment opportunities of the new area.

c) better economic possibilities.

d) Better facilities of education, housing and medical treatment.

e) Better economic prosperity, higher standard of living and better climatic conditions.

Some of the push factors involved in migration are:

1) Inadequate facilities for earning livelihood, lower wages at the existing places of living.

2) Poverty, unemployment, under-employment and low standrad of living.

3) Discrimination based on religion and politics.

4) Lack of personal development, employment and matrimonial prospect for certain groups of people.

5) Dissatisfaction with existing traditions and customs superstitions and behaviour of people.

Migration among Gonds of Behanga

Of all kinds of migration that due to marriage is the highest. Marriages involve the movement of people invariably. Such movements may be intra-village, inter-village, intra district or inter-district. Among the Gond population, movements are localised due to the universal fear of the strange, and the unknown. All Indian tribes are endogamous. Clan exogamy is the norm while tribe exogamy is tabooed in the selection of males by different clans of Gonds.

The role of migration other than marriage-migration in the demographic profile of the village has been negligible. Gond of the village are far more dependent on agriculture and forestry than any other segment of the society. But the agricultural conditions are miserably poor. They are heavily dependent on agriculture which is still operated with primitive tools and equipment. Besides, agriculture in Behanga is subject to vagaries of monsoon, the irrigation facilities being almost absent. Due to poor performance in agriculture the people of Behanga are very poor. They cannot manage for two square meals a day for themselves. They connot really think of moving from one place to another which requires money. Moreover they also do not have any specialised skill to get easy employment. Apart from this in Gonds, evils of drinking and smoking is intense whish has made them lazy. In the total population investigated (i.e. 474) the migration other than marriage migration is not there. Also, the percentage of long distance marriage migration is very low.

Table 5.18

Marriage Migration in Gonds

Clan group	Total married women	Married in the same village	Married in different village	Percentage
Maravi	32	24	8	25
Warkara	19	15	4	21
Oikey	8	6	2	25
Kushram	5	4	1	20
Chai-devki	2	2	—	—
Dhumkati	1	1	—	—
Neti	9	6	3	33.3
Partai	12	8	4	33.3
Wayam	2	2	—	—
Sriyam	5	4	1	20
Sat-devki	4	3	1	25
Sirsam	1	1	—	—
Kurwati	3	2	1	33.3
Total	103	78	25	Mean= 24.2

Table 5.18 shows that the total percentage of marriage migration is 24.2. Maximum migration is shown in Neti, Kurwati and Partai sub-tribes and no migration is recorded in sub tribes Sirsam, Dhumkati, Wayam and Chai-devki

MARRIAGE

Marriage is more than simply a legalised sexual union between a man and a woman, though it is almost always this, if we mean by 'legalised' socially acknowledged and approved.

Notes and Queries in Anthropology (1971), gives a useful preliminary definition—marriage is "a union between a man and a woman such that the children born to the woman are the recognised legitimate offspring of both partners". This points to one important function of marriage in most societies. The fact that it confers acknowledged social status on the offspring. This is evidently a matter of great importance in regard to such matters as inheritance and succession.

But their is no general definition of marriage which would include all kinds of institutionalised inter-presonal relationships. Here as so often we have to avoid the danger of uncritically assimilating other people's social and cultural institutions to our own. It is sometimes hard to decide whether a particular kind of union in a particular society can usefully be called marriage. Although the names we give to the institutions we identify are important for the purpose of thinking and communicating about them yet the first and the most important thing is to understand their nature and significance in their proper contexts.

Among the Gonds, the woman is regarded as an economic asset to the family due to her capacity to co-operate in the economic activities of her husband. The agricultural activities are mainly dependent on the co-operation of the wife, who renders better services than hired servants.

Gonds believe that a person's soul neither goes to heaven nor rests in peace if he has not married a virgin. But those who do not find virgins at times marry widows or divorced women (Yadav, 1968).

When a Gond man marries second time, no elaborate ceremonies are observed. An elderly woman of the house performs a ceremony of *haldi-dalna* and *churi-pahanana.* A second wife can be brought in the presence of first wife, or after the death of first wife or after divorce. This ceremony is called as *Char bathana.*

Although polygyny is freely allowed in the village and a Gond male may have as many wives as he can afford. Yet Gond consider monogamy as the ideal type and prefer to have only one wife at a given moment of time except in certain ex-

excptional circumstances, for example, cases where the wife is barren.

In the village out of 257 males, 21 (8.17%) had 2 wives, of which 9 had married twice because the first wife had no issue.

A Gond is expected to marry his cross-cousin except in certain circumstances. Strict adherence to this custom results in many unhappy unions, elopements and divorces in the community.

Cross cousin marriage is locally termed as *doodh-lautana*, while literally meaning, 'to return the milk'—an act of reciprocity on the part of an individual, among the Gonds. The custom has strong socio-religious force behind it. Thus, a Gond male may marry either his mother's brother's daughter (MoBoDa) on father's-sister' sdaughter (Fa Si Da). Marriage with mother's-brother's-daughter is called as *doodh-duhani-vivah* and with father's sister's daughter as *Pal-duhani vivah*.

While cross cousin marriage is preferred, the incidence of any parallel cousin marriage has not been observed. Patriarhcy prevails in this community and child marriage is still prevalent, though at a lower ebb.

The Gonds believe in a number of Gods (*Dev*) like *Teendevki*, *Chardevki*, *Panchdevki*, *Chaidevki* and *Satdevki*—which are considered as sub-totemic on sub-clan groups. Clan worshipping with sub totem, for example *chaidevki* constitute one *samdhan* (a corporate group) and has to seek spouses for their sons and daughters from the clan of another *samdhan* group. The members of one *samdhan* group refer each other as brothers and sisters. Hence, a marriage between them is a social taboo. If such a union takes place, it is considered a breach of incest taboo by the community and the couple is ostracised by he villagers.

An analysis reveals that out of 474 individuals, 106 i.e., 18% have married their cross cousins (father's-sister's daughters or sons). Besides their total adherence to this custom, the

Gonds also give several other reasons in favour of the practice of cross-cousin marriage. Some of them are :

i) Cross-cousin marriage interlaces two families and at the time of crisis both the families stand as one for defence.

ii) Parents need not worry about the marriage of their children as they (children) are to be married with their cross-cousin spouse and as such no middleman is required to settle the marriages.

iii) Since both the cross-cousins are familiar with each other from their childhood, they do not find it difficult to moke adjustments after marriage.

iv) If there is discord and a woman runs away after marriage or a man deserts his wife, both the families put pressure on the man and woman for re-union.

v) If any of the parties is not in a position to meet the marriage expenses, one can easily ask the other either for help or for postponement of marriage for some time.

Marriage distance

Gonds, prefer village endogamy and marry in the same village and if they are required to go outside, they select spouses from the village at shorter distances that can easily be covered both ways in a day. In the present study it is seen that the maximum distance where the girl is married from the village is between 10-15 km.

Such a geographical latitude of Gonds provides them full knowledge about their family. Moreover, being poor they connot afford to spend money on buses or any other modeof transport to meet their daughters. Hence, they walk down to do so. Thus, if the distances are more they will never be able to meet their daughters or the daughter will never be able to come to meet her parents.

Types of Marriage

Various types of marriages recognised by Gonds are :

Marriage by elopement (Bhagel Shadi)

An unmarried Gond girl of the age group sixteen to eighteen years of age can conveniently run away to another village with her lover who does not belong to her own clan or a clan which does not worship equal number of Gods or does not belong to either tribe falling outside the permissible limit. Later, their marriage is ritually solemnised by the parents of both parties. In such cases, the usual bride price is not paid by the bridegroom's parents to the bride's parents. At times, this type of marriage is encouraged to do away with the high cost of bride price.

Marriage by intrusion (Karel Shadi)

In this marriage an unmarried Gond girl can, with the due consent of her lover, enter his house at will and is declared as his wife. Such marriages are regularised by the Tribe Council by imposing a fine ranging from Rs. 1.50 to 150. The only condition laid down is that this act should be within the permitted rules of tribal endogamy and clan.

Marriage by exchange (Ata-sata Shadi)

This is a type of marriage by service whieh is practised popularly by those Gonds who generally cannot afford to pay bride price.

Marriage of umarried mother

In case of the premarital relation of a girl with a person falling within the permissible degree of marriage, the man is asked to accept the unmarried mother as his wife by the community panchayat. Their marrige is thus regularised. If the premarital relation happens to be with a person belonging to other caste or tribal group the unmarried mother is excommunicated by the panchayat. Parents of such a woman, however, can be re-accepted by the community after due purification. This process involves *Ganga Snana* an *Narmada Snana* and community feast. Return to her parental tribal group is impossible by a Gond woman for such a societal violation.

Widow remarriage (Bithai ohadi)

A Gond woman is permitted to opt for a remarriage of her choice. The choice may be for a bachelor on a widower. However, the first claim on such widow for rmarriage is vested with the *dewar* i.e. immediate younger brother of the deceased husband.

Divorce

The frequency of divorce is high, mainly because of unsuccessful cross cousin marriage. In the village about 6% per cent of the total populatiou have ended in a divorce.

Divorce brings gains to no one but it certainly causes the loss of prestige to all those concerned. It effects the economy of husband's family quite severely because a woman among Gond is of a very great help in agriculture.

Divorce in Gonds is common and easy, and does not require any legal sanction. The Gonds allow divorce freely on grounds of marital infidelity, carelessness in household work, barrenness and quarrelsome disposition.

If a woman goes to the Panchayat for divorce then her husband has to pay *Dava* i.e. a small price, say 200-300 rupees or a small piece of land in compensation.

6

Summary

A demographic profile of Behanga, a village in Mandla district of Madhya Pradesh, has been attempted in this study. Mandla is situated almost in the centre of Madhya Pradesh at the height of 1200-1400 ft. Jabalpur and Shahdol districts are situated on the northern part of Mandla. The eastern border of Mandla is covered by Bilaspur and Rajnandgao districts. On the southern border is Balaghat district while western part is covered by Sivini districts. The total population of Mandla block according to 1981 census is 10, 36, 134, out of which 6, 21, 051 population i.e. 59.94% is tribal. Whereas, 85% of the total tribal population consists of Gond population.

The area investigated was economically backward, illiterate and poverty stricken. It was hypothesised as under.

—Number of males and females shall be nearly equal with males outnumbering females at younger age and females outnumbering the males from about the age of 20-25 onwards, the overall effect being that the females outnumber males to a certain extent.

—The fertility rate is expected to be high.

—Mortality rate and infant mortality rates are expected to be high.

—Internal migration, especially inter-state movement shall be minimal. Marriage migration shall be the only way of territorial mobility, extended within a specified short distance.

—The knowledge of family planning and the means of adoption is expected to be lower.

The data were collected from the selected households after simple random sampling by administering schedule. The unit of enquiry i.e. "household" meant all members in a house, who had a common kitchen (*chullah*) and who lived under one roof.

Besides, the method of Schedule and observations, method of interview were also adopted to seek additional information on economic status, family planning and various other aspects.

The population of the village constitute of Gond population. In all, their are 102 households in the village constituting of 813 persons. The total number of households investigated by the investigator was 69 constituting of 474 persons.

The density of population recorded in Mandla district is 78 persons per sq km and male female ratios is 1:1. The Gond population is divided into, number of clans. These clans are usually named after animals and plants. For example *Markam* (mango tree), *Warkara* (wild cat) etc. These animals and plants from which a clan derives its names are totems for the members of the social group.

The sex ratio (according to census report 1981) of India is 933 and that of Madhya Pradesh is 941. Whereas the sex ratio in the present analysis is found to be 919. According to age and sex structure of the village, maximum population density indicated in the age group 0—4 years and sex ratio of the group is 789.5. The economically active group i.e. 15-59 years consists of 278 persons out of which 142 are males and 136 are females. Economically in active group i.e. 0-15 and 60+ consist of 195 persons.

The dependency ratio of India, Madhya Pradesh and Gonds of Behanga were found to 83.2, 97.89 and 69.89 r espectively. Thus, the dependency ratios of the village is the least.

The total number of males and females within the age groups 0-20 years constitute of 124 males and 115 females and above 20 the number of males is 123 and females is 112, which shows that the male population is dominant in the village. Hence, the first hypothesis that number of males and females shall be nearly equal with males outnumbering females at a younger age and females outnumbering the males from about the age of 20-25 onwards, the over all effect being the females outnumber males to a certain extent stands invalid.

An investigation of distribution of village population with respect to marital status reveals that the number of married individuals is 182 consisting of 88 males and 94 females. Unmarried individuals are 240 consisting of 130 males and 110 females. The number of widows, widowers and divorced males and females are 18, 5, 17 and 12 respectively.

A comparative account of Mean age at marriage of different clans of Gonds show that mean age of marriage for girls is 16 years and for boys it is 19 years. In our present analysis it is found that Gonds prefer village endogamy and clan exogamy. The maximum distance of marriage is 10-15 km.

The primary occupation of the Gonds is agriculture. More than 93% of the Gond population is dependent on agriculture.

whereas, rest are involved in jobs like teaching, forest service or are labourers etc.

Literacy rate of the Gond population is found to be very low. 77.6% of the total population are illiterates. There are no graduates or post-graduates in the village.

In the village nuclear family system is more prevalent. 78.26% families are nuclear families and 21.73% have extended famllles. The size of the family varies from 2 to 20 members. The actual and the preferred family size are varying. The actual family size is 5-6 while preferred is 3-4.

According to the hypothesis it is expected that the birth-rates of the Gond population should be high. The birth rates of India, Madhya Pradesh and Gonds in Behanga village are found to be 33.3, 38.5 and 42.19 respectively. Thus, the birth rate in the village is found to be high and hence our hypothesis stands valid.

Mortality rate and infant mortality rates are high in the village. The crude death rate is 40.08 and infant mortality rate being 242.4. The infant deaths recorded in the study are neo-natal and post-natal deaths. These deaths are assigned to exogenous factors like infection, diseases, climatic conditions etc. Hence, our second hypothesis that mortality and infant mortality rates shall be high stands valid.

The survey reveals that the people are quite aware of the family planning programmes although the application of the contraception is restricted to a limited number of the couples. 42% of couples use various contraceptive devices but even more couples express their desire of having a few children but the lack of education and general notion that children are the gift of God or His will become the impediments in the effectiveness and acceptance of family planning programmes. It is to be mentioned that since the people are aware of the troubles of having large families they can be expected to alter and modify in future their attitudes towards family planning. Thus, our third hypothesis does stand valid.

Migration in the village is nil. The only type of migration recorded is the marriage migration. The total percentage of marriage migration is 24.2. Hence our 4th hypothesis that internal migration especially interstate movement shall be minimal and marriage migration shall be the only way of migration stands valid.

To sum up, it may be pointed out that the Gond population, under study, shows the characteristics, typical of the first stage of Demographic Transition, where a high birth rate is matched by a high death rate. The incidence of death is high owing to poor diet and malnutrition, inadequate medical facilities to curb high infant mortality and mortality in general. Poor sanitation and unhygienic conditions are prevalent. Looking at the causes of death (malaria, infections of stomach, cough etc). one is forced to believe that the infections responsible for mortality are owing to improper, unhygienic living conditions in Gond population, which must be improved by the concerned authorities so that the death rate is brought to a bare minimum if not at par with the all India death rate (12.5 persons per 1000) in 1981.

The birth rate is also high because the death rate is high. The population cannot perpetuate and thrive unless the birth rate is made correspondingly high. In a society like Gond where paternity is glorified and a woman with a number of children is held in high esteem, the cultural factors contribute significantly towards a high birth rate. Children are considered assets in the family. Economic baekwardness, lack of formal education and poverty contribute to maintain a high birth rate. Hoever, there is a general awareness and motivation now towards methods of family planning and couples are resorting to the different methods of contraception. There is no territorial movement of the members of Gond population excepting the marriage migration—another characteristic feature of population in first stage of demographic transition.

As a result of high birth rate and high death rate there is a corresponding low and stable population growth in Gonds, which is a characteristic of all populations belonging to the first stage of transition (like population of some African countries). With the economie development, which may have direct and indirect economic changes, the most important of which is the availability of improved medical facilities, better quality food products, balanced diet, good drinking water, proper sanitation and hygienic conditions, we expect a fall in death rate in Gond population. According to the Demographic Transition Theory the corresponding birth rate would also decline, though slowly, paving the way for the third stage of slow and stationary population, typical of the population of advanced nations.

Selected Bibliography

Aggarwal, S.N. 1973. *India's Population Problems*, New Delhi: Tata Mc Graw. Hill Publishing Co. Ltd.

Ashfaq, A.S. 1973. *Tribal Demography of Madhya Pradesh*, Bhopal : Jai Bharat Publishing House.

Beattie, J., 1972. *Other Cultures*, London : Routledge and Kegan Paul Co. Ltd.

Bose, A., A. Mitra., P.B. Desai., J.N. Sharma, (editors). *Population in India's Development 1947-2000*. Delhi : Vikas Publishing House.

Bose, A., D.B. Gupta. M.K. Premi, (editors), 1982. *Social Statistics : Health and Education*. New Delhi : Vikas Publishing House.

Bumpass, L. and C.F. Westoff. Cited from *Demography, A Status Study on Population Research in India* (Vol. II), New Delhi : Tata Mc Graw Hill Publishing House.

Cannan, R, 1916. *Wealth*. Orchard House : P.S. Kings and Sons, Ltd.

Carr-Saunder, A.M. 1926 *Eugenics*. London : Thornaton Butterworth Limited.

Cassen, R.H. 1982. *India's Population, Economy and Society*, London : The Macmillan Press, Ltd.

Chandna, R.C. 1986, *A Geography of Population*, New Delhi: Kalyani Publishers.

Chandrasekhar, S. 1972, *Infant Mortality, Population Growth and Family Planning in India*, London : George Allen and Unwin, Ltd.

Cowgill, D.O. 1949. The Theory of Population Growth Cycles, *The American Journal of Sociology*, 55:17-18.

Cox, P.R. 1976 *Demography*, Cambridge: University Press.

Danda, A.K. 1984. *Family Planning—An Adaptive Strategy*. New Delhi : Inter-India Publications.

Dell, B.N., G.F. Luthringer. 1938. *Population Resources and Trade* (Vol. V), Boston: Litttle Brown and Co.

Dubey, B.R. 1968. "Widow Remarriage in Madhya Pradesh". *Man in India*. 45:50-57.

Dumont, A. 1957. *Population Theories and the Economics Interpretation*, London : Routledge and` Kegan Paul Ltd.

Fetter, F. 1957. *Population Theories and the Economics Interpretation*, London : Routledge and Kegan Paul, Ltd.

Fuchs, S. 1960. *Bhumia Gonds of Eastern Mandla*, Bombay: Asia Publishing House.

Ghosh, B.N. 1983. *Population Theories and Demographic Analysis*. Meerut : Meenakshi Prakashan.

Government of India. 1985. *Child In India, A Statistical Profile*, New Delhi : Ministry of Welfare.

Guillard, A. 1855. Cited from, *An Introduction to Social Demography*, Delhi: Vikas Publishing House, Pvt. Ltd.

Hussain, I.Z. 1972. Cited from, *Demographic Structure of Tribal Society*, Meerut : Meenakshi Prakashan.

India, A Reference Annual. 1983. *India 1983*, New Delhi : Ministry of Information and Broadcasting.

Jain, S.P. 1975. *Demography., A Status Study on Population Research in India* (Vol. II), New Delhi : Tata McGraw-Hill Publishing Co.

Jaiswal, H.K. 1979. *Demographic Structure of Tribal Society*, Meerut : Meenakshi Prakashan.

Kaul, S. and Amita Kala. 1977. "Fertility and Family Planning in a Remote Hill Area of Himachal Pradesh", *The Journal of Family Welfare*, 33:3.

Kohli, K.L. 1977. *Mortality in India*, Delhi: Sterling Publishers, Pvt. Ltd.

Krech, David and Crutchfield, R.S. 1948. *Theory and Problems of Social Psychology*, New York: Mc Graw Hill Book Company.

Leibenstein, H. 1954. *A Theory of Economic Demographic Developmant*, Princeton : Princeton University Press.

Malthus, T. Robert. 1894, *Essays on the Principle of Population*, London : Mcamillan and Company.

Marx, K. Cited from, *Text Book of Demography*, New Delhi : Vikas Publishing House.

Mathur, R.N. 1986. *Population-Analysis and Studies*, Allahabad : Chugh Publications.

Mehta, B.H. 1984. *Gonds of the Central India Highlands* (Vol. I), New Delhi: Concept Publishing House.

Nitti, F.S. Cited from, *Dynamics of Population Growth*, Lucknow : Joytsna Publications.

Patel, M.L. 1985: "Customary Laws Among Gonds of Madhya Pradesh", Human Science, 34:5-17.

Premi, M.K., A Ramanamma., Usha Bambawale, E. (edtiors), 1983. *An Introduction to Social Demography.* Delhi: Vikas Publishing House Pvt Ltd.

Raizada, A. 1984 *Tribal Development in Madhya Pradesh—A Planning Perspective.* New Delhi : Inter—India Publications.

Raj, H. 1978. *Fundamentals of Demography,* Delhi : Surjit Book House.

Robbins, L. 1927. *Eassays in Economics in Honour of Edwin Cannan,* London: Routledge and Kegan Paul.

Royal Anthropological Institute of Great Britain and Ireland. 1971. *Notes and Queries on Anthropology,* London : Routledge and Kegan Paul. Ltd.

Russel, R.V. and Hira Lal. 1975, *Tribes and Castes of Central Provinces of India* (Vol. III), Delhi : Rajdhani Book Centre.

Sax, K. 1950. *The Population Explosion,* Headline Series 120, Foreign Policy Association.

Shrivastava, O.S. 1983. *A Text Book of Demography,* Delhi : Vikas Publishing House Pvt. Ltd.

Spengler, J.J. and D.D. Duncan. 1956 : *Population Theory and Policy* Glencoe Illionois : The Free Press.

Spiegal, M.R. 1975. *Theory and Problems of Statistics,* New Delhi : Tata Mc Graw Hill Publishing Company. Pvt. Ltd.

Srinivashan, K. and S. Mukerji, 1981. *Dynamics of Population and Family Welfare.* Bombay : Himalaya Publishing House.

Thompson, W.S. and D.T. Lewis, 1965. *Population Problems,* New Delhi: Tata Mc Graw Hill Publishing Company.

Verma, J.M. 1977. *Dynamics of Population Growth*, Lucknow: Jyotsna Publications.

Vig, O.P. 1976. *India's Population*, New Delhi : Sterling Publishers Pvt. Ltd.

Yadav, K.S. 1968. "Gonds Cross-Cousin Marriage", *Man in India*, 50:289-97.

Appendix

SCHEDULE

1) Name of the head of the household : ....

2) Name of the respondent : ....

3) Age : .... 4) Sex :......................

5) Marital Status : ....

6) a) Occupation : ....

b) Distance (in case of persons point out of the village) :- : ....

7) Education : .... :..................

8) Religion : ....

9) Caste.........................10) Sub-caste...............

11) canguage

Family Composition :

S. No.	Name	Relation with head of Household	Age	Sex	Marital status	Children	Education	Occupation	Income

12 Marriage :

a) S. No.	Age of Marriage		No. of children.	Age
	Wife	Husband		

(b What is the ideal age in your opinion for marriage Male................ Female..............

c) How do you arrange your marriage :- Through parents/relatives/employment/purchase/choice/exchange/any other
Reasons :...

d) Do you have any restrictions on widow re-marriage- Yes/No
Reasons : ....

e) Do you have any restrictions on widower re-marriage : Yes/No
Reasons : ....

f) Is dowry system prevalent in your community:- Yes/No
If yes. to what extent..........................

g) Has the husband any access to his wife before marriage both in terms of gifts of sex :— Yes/No
Reasons :.................................

h) Has any person in your family married with more than one women. If yes how many :.......................

i) In your eommunity can a woman marry with more than one man (Polyandry). If yes, reasons : ....

j) Can a person have the right to establish sex relationship besides his legal wife in your community.
Reasons : ....

k) Can a woman have the right to establish sex relation besides her legal husband. If yes, give reasons...........

l) Whether cross cousin or parallel cousin marriage prevalent in your community.
Reasons :.....................................

m) Distance of marriage : ....

n) Age at first couplation and Puberty : ....

13) Fertility History :—

S. No.	Age at which pregnancy took place	Result of conception L.B.	S.B.	Misca-rriage	Abo-rtion	If not alive age at death

14 a) Do you know that you can space in between 2 children and limit the size of family by using artificial means. Yes/No

b) Do you approve this method. Yes/No

c) Have you used any means to space between the children or avoid conception. Yes/No

15 a) If yes what method did you use....................

b) How did you come to know : ....

c) Are you still continuing the use of any method : Yes/No

if yes which one and why : ....

16 Do you have any institution/dispensary to guide you in this matter : ....

17 a) In your opinion what would be the ideal size of family.
Children...............Male...........Female............

b) Reasons for high or low fertility :.................

18 What is the number live births within last one year.

19 Whether the child births take place at in-law's place or natal family :

20 Whether the child birth takes place at dispensary/mid-wife, hospital/home. Reasons : ....

21 Upto what time is the concept of breast feeding prevalent : ....

22 How much is the period of rest after child birth and various restrictions for the mother : ....

23 **Mortality :-**

During the last five years has there been any death in your family. If yes, furnish the information.

Name	Relation	Age	Sex	Cause	Treatment	Occupation	Income

24 **Migration :**

a) What is your birth place :....................

b) Are you permanent settler of this area. Yes/No......

c) If yes, for how long....................

d) If no, the place of last residence ....

25. Can you give the reasons for choosing this particular village for residence..........................

26 What was the occupation of migrant before migration

27 Do you consider yourself to be adequately rehabited give reasons : ....

28 Whether the migration is from :-

1) Village to village : ....
2) Village to State : ....
3) Village to countries : ....
4) Village to city : ....

29 (a) Is there any pull factor acting far migration: Yes/No Reason....... ....

(b) Is there any push factor acting for the migration. Yes/No

Reasons : ....

30 Any other information : ....

APPENDIX -II

TABLE SHOWING

CLAN WISE DISTRIBUTION OF GOND POPULATION IN BEHANGA BY AGE AND SEX

CLAN/SUB TRIBE		AGE GROUP 0-4	5-9	10-14	15-19	20-24	25-29	30-34	35-39	40-44	45-49	50-54	55-59	60+	Total
WARAKARA	Males	5	11	10	7	4	2	2	4	4	2	2	-	2	55
	Females	4	5	5	4	6	4	3	4	2	3	1	1	-	42
	Total	9	16	15	11	10	6	5	8	6	5	3	1	2	97
	Sex ratio	800	455	500	571	1500	2000	1500	1000	500	1500	500	0	0	764
MARAVI	M	8	10	9	6	3	4	2	7	5	1	3	3	1	62
	F	6	5	11	10	7	4	3	3	3	4	3	1	2	62
	T	14	15	20	16	10	8	5	10	8	5	6	4	3	124
	Sex ratio	750	500	1222	1667	2333	1000	1500	429	600	4000	1000	333	2000	1000
PARTAI	M	4	3	6	4	3	2	2	3	1	2	1	-	2	33
	F	7	7	2	3	2	4	2	1	-	-	-	-	1	30
	T	11	10	8	7	5	6	4	4	1	2	1	-	3	63
	Sex ratio	1750	2333	333	750	667	2000	1000	250	-	-	-	-	500	909
NETI	M	3	3	2	4	1	2	4	-	3	2	1	1	-	26
	F	1	5	3	2	2	2	-	3	1	-	-	-	1	20
	T	4	8	5	6	3	4	4	3	4	2	1	1	1	46
	Sex ratio	333	1667	1500	500	2000	1000	-	-	333	-	-	-	-	769
OIKEY	M	3	3	4	-	1	3	-	2	1	1	-	1	-	19
	F	1	2	5	2	3	3	2	2	-	1	1	-	-	22
	T	4	5	9	2	4	6	2	4	1	2	1	1	-	41
	Sex ratio	333	667	1250	-	3000	1000	-	1000	-	1000	-	-	-	1158
KUSHRAM	M	-	3	2	2	2	3	1	-	-	-	1	-	1	15
	F	-	2	-	2	1	-	-	-	-	1	-	1	-	7
	T	-	5	2	4	3	3	1	-	-	1	1	1	1	22
	Sex ratio	-	667	-	1000	500	-	-	-	-	-	-	-	-	467
DHUMKATI	M	1	-	-	-	1	-	1	-	-	-	-	1	-	4
	F	-	2	2	-	1	1	-	-	-	-	1	-	-	7
	T	1	2	2	-	2	1	1	-	-	-	1	1	-	11
	Sex ratio	-	-	-	-	1000	-	-	-	-	-	-	-	-	1750
CHAI-DEVKI	M	1	1	1	-	-	1	-	-	1	-	-	-	-	5
	F	-	1	1	1	-	1	-	-	-	1	-	-	-	5
	T	1	2	2	1	-	2	-	-	1	1	-	-	-	10
	Sex ratio	-	1000	1000	-	-	1000	-	-	-	-	-	-	-	1000
WAYAM	M	-	-	-	1	-	1	2	-	-	1	-	1	-	6
	F	-	-	1	1	1	-	1	-	-	-	-	-	-	5
	T	-	-	1	2	1	1	3	-	-	1	-	1	-	11
	Sex ratio	-	-	-	1000	-	-	500	-	-	-	-	-	-	833
SARIYAM	M	2	2	-	1	1	1	-	-	-	-	-	-	1	8
	F	1	2	-	-	1	1	-	-	-	-	-	-	-	5
	T	3	4	-	1	2	2	-	-	-	-	-	1	-	13
	Sex ratio	500	1000	-	1000	1000	-	-	-	-	-	-	-	-	625
SIRSAM	M	1	1	1	-	-	-	-	1	-	-	-	-	1	5
	F	1	1	-	-	-	1	-	-	-	-	-	1	-	4
	T	2	2	1	-	-	1	-	1	-	-	-	1	1	9
	Sex ratio	1000	1000	-	-	-	-	-	-	-	-	-	-	-	800
KURWATI	M	-	-	-	2	1	1	1	-	-	-	1	-	-	6
	F	-	-	1	1	1	-	-	-	-	1	-	-	-	4
	T	[illegible]	-	1	3	2	1	1	-	-	1	-	-	-	10
	Sex ratio	[illegible]	-	-	500	1000	-	-	-	-	-	-	-	-	667
SAT-DEVKI	M	1	-	2	2	1	-	-	1	-	-	-	-	-	8
	F	-	1	1	1	-	-	1	-	-	1	-	-	-	5
	T	1	1	3	3	1	-	1	1	-	1	-	-	-	13
	Sex ratio	-	-	500	500	-	-	-	-	-	-	-	-	-	625

APPENDIX-II

TABLE SHOWING

CLAN-WISE MARITAL STATUS OF GOND POPULATION IN BEHANGA

CLAN/SUB-TRIBES		AGE GROUPS 0-9 M	0-9 F	10-14 M	10-14 F	15-19 M	15-19 F	20-24 M	20-24 F	25-29 M	25-29 F	30-34 M	30-34 F	35-39 M	35-39 F	40-44 M	40-44 F	45-49 M	45-49 F	50-54 F	50-54 M	55-59 M	55-59 F	60+ M	60+ F	Total M	Total F
	Married	-	-	-	1	1	2	2	2	3	3	4	3	3	2	3	2	1	3	1	1	1	-	-	-	21	21
MARAVI	Unmarried	19	15	6	3	6	1	2	-	1	-	-	-	-	-	-	-	-	-	-	-	-	-	-	-	34	19
	Widow	-	-	-	-	-	-	-	-	-	-	-	1	-	-	-	-	-	1	-	-	-	-	-	-	-	2
	Widower	-	-	-	-	-	-	-	-	-	-	-	-	-	-	-	-	-	-	-	-	-	-	-	-	-	-
	Divorce	-	-	-	-	-	-	-	-	-	1	-	-	1	-	-	-	1	-	-	-	-	-	-	-	2	-
	Married	-	-	-	1	1	3	5	4	4	7	2	2	2	1	1	-	1	1	-	1	1	-	-	-	17	20
WARKARA	Unmarried	3	15	5	3	3	1	1	1	-	-	-	-	-	-	-	-	-	-	-	-	-	-	-	-	22	20
	Widow	-	-	-	-	-	-	-	-	-	1	-	1	-	-	-	-	-	1	-	-	-	-	-	1	-	3
	Widower	-	-	-	-	-	-	-	-	-	-	-	-	-	-	-	-	-	-	-	-	1	-	-	-	1	-
	Divorce	-	-	-	-	-	-	-	-	1	-	-	1	-	-	1	-	-	-	-	-	-	-	-	-	2	1
	Married	-	-	-	1	1	2	1	2	1	2	2	2	1	2	1	-	2	1	1	2	2	1	1	-	13	16
PARTAI	Unmarried	9	9	5	3	3	4	4	1	1	-	-	-	-	-	-	-	-	-	-	-	-	-	-	-	22	17
	Widow	-	-	-	-	-	-	-	-	-	1	-	-	-	-	-	1	-	-	-	-	-	-	-	1	-	3
	Widower	-	-	-	-	-	-	-	-	-	-	-	-	-	-	-	-	-	-	-	-	1	-	-	-	1	-
	Divorce	-	-	-	-	-	-	-	-	-	-	-	1	1	-	-	-	-	-	1	-	-	-	-	-	3	1
	Married	-	-	-	-	3	3	2	2	2	2	-	-	1	1	1	2	1	-	-	1	-	-	-	-	10	10
NETI	Unmarried	13	12	7	9	3	4	2	1	1	-	-	-	-	-	-	-	-	-	-	-	-	-	-	-	26	26
	Widow	-	-	-	-	-	-	-	1	-	-	-	-	-	-	-	-	-	1	-	-	-	-	-	-	-	7
	Widower	-	-	-	-	-	-	-	-	-	-	-	-	-	-	-	-	-	-	-	-	-	-	-	-	-	-
	Divorce	-	-	-	-	-	-	-	-	-	-	-	-	1	1	1	-	-	-	1	-	-	-	-	-	3	1
	Married	-	-	-	2	1	-	1	1	2	2	1	1	1	-	-	1	1	1	1	-	1	1	1	1	10	10
OIKEY	Unmarried	3	5	4	4	2	5	2	2	1	-	-	-	-	-	-	-	-	-	-	-	-	-	-	-	12	10
	Widow	-	-	-	-	-	-	-	-	-	-	-	1	-	-	-	-	-	-	-	1	-	-	-	-	-	2
	Widower	-	-	-	-	-	-	-	-	-	-	-	-	-	-	-	-	-	-	-	-	-	-	1	-	1	-
	Divorce	-	-	-	-	-	-	-	1	-	-	-	1	1	-	-	1	-	-	-	-	-	-	-	-	1	3
	Married	-	-	-	1	1	2	-	-	1	-	-	-	-	-	-	1	-	-	1	1	-	-	-	-	5	5
KUSHRAM	Unmarried	1	1	1	1	1	-	1	-	-	-	-	-	-	-	-	-	-	-	-	-	-	-	-	-	4	2
	Widow	-	-	-	-	-	-	-	-	-	1	-	-	-	-	-	-	-	-	-	-	-	-	-	-	-	1
	Widower	-	-	-	-	-	-	-	-	-	-	-	-	-	-	-	-	-	-	-	-	-	-	-	-	-	-
	Divorce	-	-	-	-	-	-	-	-	-	1	-	-	-	-	-	-	-	-	-	-	-	-	-	-	-	1
	Married	-	-	-	-	-	1	-	-	1	-	-	1	-	-	1	-	-	1	1	-	-	-	-	-	3	3
DHUMKATI	Unmarried	1	2	1	-	1	-	-	-	-	-	-	-	-	-	-	-	-	-	-	-	-	-	-	-	-	2
	Widow	-	-	-	-	-	-	-	-	-	-	-	-	-	-	-	1	-	-	-	-	-	-	-	-	-	1
	Widower	-	-	-	-	-	-	-	-	-	-	-	-	-	-	-	-	-	-	-	-	-	-	-	-	1	-
	Divorce	-	-	-	-	-	-	-	-	1	-	-	1	-	-	-	-	-	-	-	-	-	-	-	-	-	-
	Married	-	-	-	-	1	1	-	-	-	1	1	-	-	-	-	-	-	-	-	-	-	-	-	-	2	2
CHAI-DEVKI	Unmarried	1	1	-	-	-	-	-	-	-	-	-	-	-	-	-	-	-	-	-	-	-	-	-	-	1	1
	Wido	-	-	-	-	-	-	-	-	-	-	-	-	-	-	-	-	-	-	-	-	-	-	-	-	-	-
	Widower	-	-	-	-	-	-	-	-	-	-	-	-	-	-	-	-	-	-	-	-	-	-	-	-	-	-
	Divorce	-	-	-	-	-	-	-	-	-	-	1	-	-	1	-	-	-	-	-	-	-	-	-	-	1	1
	Married	-	-	-	-	-	2	-	1	-	1	-	-	1	-	-	1	-	-	-	-	-	-	-	-	3	3
WAYAM	Unmarried	1	-	-	1	-	-	-	-	-	-	-	-	-	-	-	-	-	-	-	-	-	-	-	-	1	1
	Widow	-	-	-	-	-	-	-	-	-	-	-	-	-	-	-	-	-	-	-	-	-	-	-	-	-	-
	Widower	-	-	-	-	-	-	-	-	-	-	-	-	-	-	-	-	-	-	-	-	-	-	-	-	-	-
	Divorce	-	-	-	-	-	-	-	1	-	-	-	-	1	-	-	-	-	-	-	-	-	-	-	-	1	1
	Married	-	-	-	-	-	1	-	-	1	-	-	-	-	-	-	-	-	-	-	-	-	-	-	-	1	1
SARIYAM	Unmarried	-	1	-	-	-	-	-	-	-	-	-	-	-	-	-	-	-	-	-	-	-	-	-	-	-	1
	Widow	-	-	-	-	-	-	-	-	-	-	-	1	-	-	-	-	-	-	-	-	-	-	-	-	-	1
	Widower	-	-	-	-	-	-	-	-	-	-	-	-	-	-	-	-	-	-	-	-	-	-	-	-	-	-
	Divorce	-	-	-	-	-	-	-	-	1	-	-	-	-	-	-	-	-	-	-	-	-	-	-	-	1	-
	Married	-	-	-	-	-	-	1	1	-	-	-	-	-	-	-	-	-	-	-	-	-	-	-	-	1	1
SIRSAM	Unmarried	-	1	-	1	-	-	-	1	-	-	-	-	-	-	-	-	-	-	-	-	-	-	-	-	-	3
	Widow	-	-	-	-	-	-	-	-	-	-	-	-	-	-	-	-	-	-	-	-	-	-	-	-	-	1
	Widower	-	-	-	-	-	-	-	-	-	-	-	-	-	-	-	-	-	-	-	-	-	-	-	-	-	-
	Divorce	-	-	-	-	-	-	-	-	-	-	-	-	-	-	-	-	-	-	-	-	-	-	-	-	-	-
	Married	-	-	-	-	-	1	-	-	-	-	-	-	1	-	-	-	-	-	-	-	-	-	-	-	1	1
KURWATI	Unmarried	1	1	1	-	-	-	-	-	-	-	-	-	-	-	-	-	-	-	-	-	-	-	-	-	3	1
	Widow	-	-	-	-	-	-	-	-	-	-	-	-	-	-	-	-	-	-	-	-	-	-	-	-	-	-
	Widower	-	-	-	-	-	-	-	-	-	-	-	-	-	-	-	-	-	-	-	-	-	-	-	-	-	-
	Divorce	-	-	-	-	-	-	-	-	-	-	-	-	1	-	-	-	-	-	-	-	-	-	-	-	1	-
	Married	-	-	-	1	-	-	1	-	-	-	-	-	-	-	-	-	-	-	-	-	-	-	-	-	1	1
SAT-DEVKI	Unmarried	1	1	1	1	-	-	-	-	-	-	-	-	-	-	-	-	-	-	-	-	-	-	-	-	2	2
	Widow	-	-	-	-	-	-	-	-	-	-	-	-	-	-	-	-	1	-	-	-	-	-	-	-	-	-
	Widower	-	-	-	-	-	-	-	-	-	-	-	-	-	-	-	-	-	-	-	-	-	-	-	-	-	[illegible]
	Divorce	-	-	-	-	-	-	-	-	-	-	1	-	-	1	-	-	-	-	-	-	-	-	-	-	1	-

APPENDIX—III

Table—Showing

Population in India Census : 1901-1981

Year	Total Population (in lakh)			Decennial change (%)	Geometric growth rate	Sex ratio (F/Mx 1000)	Density of population per sq. km.	%of urban population to total population
	Person	Male	Female					
1901	2,384 0	1,207.9	1,73.6	—	—	972	77	10.84
1911	2,520.9	1,283.8	1,237.1	5.75	(+) 0.56	964	82	10.29
1921	2,513.2	1,285.5	1,227.7	(—)0.31	(—) 0.03	955	81	11.18
1931	2,789.8	1,429.3	1,357.9	11.0	(+) 1.06	950	90	11.18
1941	3,186.6	1,636.8	1,546.8	14.22	(+) 1.34	945	103	13.86
1951	3,610.9	1,855.3	1,755.6	13.31	(+) 1.26	946	117	17.29
1961	4,392.3	2,262.9	2,129.4	21.51	(+) 1.98	941	142	17.97
1971	5,481.6	2,840.5	2,641.1	24.80	(+) 2.24	930	177	19.91
1981	6,851.8	3,544.0	3,307.8	25.00	(+) 2.26	933	216	23.31

(Source : *Child in India*, 1985)

APPENDIX—IV

Table—Showing

Percentage Distribution of Live Births by order of Birth and area in India (General) and Madhya Pradesh (1972 and 1978)

India/State	Area	Percentage of live-births by order of birth: 1 (1972)	1 (1978)	2 (1972)	2 (1978)	3 (1972)	3 (1978)	4 (1972)	4 (1978)	5 (1972)	5 (1978)	6 (1972)	6 (1978)	Total: 7 (1972)	7 (1978)
India	Rural	19.85	23.45	17.44	20.73	15.70	17.49	13.77	13.38	11.24	9.69	22.0	13.36	100.0	100.0
	Urban	21.60	25.75	18.22	23.33	16.19	17.88	14.45	12.22	9.52	7.93	20.02	12.89	100.0	100.0
	Rural	19.89	22.35	15.16	19.22	13.58	16.29	14.72	13.26	11.13	10.25	10.25	25.52	100.0	100.0
Madhya Pradesh	Urban	19.73	21.33	15.92	22.34	17.49	18.73	16.59	14.39	11.89	8.10	8.10	17.93	100.0	100.0

(Source : *Child in India*, 1985)

APPENDIX—V

Table—Showing

Average Fertility Rate, Total Fertility Rate and Gross Reproduction Rates of India (General) and Madhya Pradesh

India/State	Area	General fertility rate		Total fertility rate		Gross reproduction rate	
		1971-73	1976-78	1979-73	1976-78	1971-73	1976-78
	All	157.3	141.9	5.0	4.6	2.5	2.2
	Rural	164.0	150.2	5.3	4.9	2.6	2.4
	Urban	130.5	111.3	4.0	3.5	1.9	1.6
	All	180.0	167.9	5.7	5.5	2.8	2.7
Madhya	Rural	187.6	175.3	6.0	5.8	2.9	2.8
Pradesh	Urban	144.8	130.5	4.5	4.1	2.4	2.0

Index

Ata-State Shadi 108
Baby-boom period 23
Bewari 65
Bhagel Shadi 108
Bidri Ceremony 45
Bithai Ohadi 109
Biyari 40
Bura Deo 31,45
Capitalistic Method of production 16
Chait Gal 45
Char-bathana 105
Clan-exogamy 30, 103, 113
Consumption utility 20
Cross-cousine Marriage 30
Dava 109
Demographic Analysis 3,47,25
Demographic Events 69
Demographic explanation 4
Demographic Process 77
Demographic Study 51
Demographic Structure 7
Demographic Transition 2, 21, 24
Density of population 29
Dependency Ratio 53, 55, 56
Dhumkati 51
Doodh Duhani Vivah 106
Doodh Lautana 106
Endogs my 103, 113
Geometrical proportions 12
Geography of Hunger 87

Geometrical proportions
Geometrical rate 16
Guria 31, 41, 45, 96
Hareli 44
Jaura 40
Karel Shadi 108
Karma 43
Karma Kalla 43
Khyania 44
Live births 98
Malthusian cycle 23
Marriya 40
Mela Madai 44
Mo-Bo-Da 106
Monogamous Marriage 30
Monogamy 105
Mukadam 32
Nawa Feast 45
Non-productive Age 20
Nuptiality 6
Optimum population 12, 13, 14,24
Pal duhani Vrah 106
Parallel-cousin 36
Patriarchy 30
Person-year 94
Polygamy 30, 60, 105
Population Composition 48
Population Epoch 23
Population Explosion 1
Productive Agent 20
Reena dance 44
Saila dance 44
Saj Tree 31
Samdhan 106
Shankar Chauth 45
Social Capillarity 16, 17
Social Demography 4 5, 6, 39
Social Cultural Economics 21
Secio-Economic Changes 36
Social Stratification 17
Sub-human existence 40
Surplus population 15
Totemic Symbol 30
Tribal endogamy 30
Tukria 44
Voluntarism 18